SOLID WASTE POLLUTION AND HEALTH

SOLID WASTE POLLUTION
AND
HEALTH

By

Prof. E.H.El.Mossalamy

Chairman/Professor
Dept. of Chemistry
Faculty of Science
King Abdul Aziz University
Jeddah, (K.S.A.)

DISCOVERY PUBLISHING HOUSE PVT. LTD.
NEW DELHI-110 002

Published by:
Tilak Wasan
DISCOVERY PUBLISHING HOUSE PVT. LTD.
4383/4B, Ansari Road, Darya Ganj
New Delhi-110 002 (India)
Phone : +91-11-23279245, 43596064-65
Fax : +91-11-23253475
E-mail : discoverypublishinghouse@gmail.com
sales@discoverypublishinggroup.com
parul.wasan@gmail.com
web : www.discoverypublishinggroup.com

***First Edition:* 2013**

ISBN: 978-93-5056-306-9

Solid Waste Pollution and Health

Printed at:
Aditi Fine Art Press
Delhi

FOREWORD

A continuous migration of peoples from rural areas to semi-urban areas, town and cities has increased more than 25 per cent in past two decades. The uncontrolled growth in urban areas has left many cities of almost every country, deficient in infrastructural services, such as water supply, sewerage and municipal solid waste management. Due to lack of serious efforts by town/city authorities garbage and its management has become tenacious problem all over the world. A continuous decline in standard of services with respect to the collection and disposal of municipal solid waste, hospital waste, industrial wastes, as well as including domestic and plastic wastes has created a serious situation of sanitation and public health. For obtaining a long term sustainable, economic solution, planning of the system on long term basis is very essential.

I congratulate **Professor Dr. E.H. El-Mossalamy,** Faculty of Sciences, Department of Chemistry, King Abdul Aziz University, Jeddah, Saudi Arabia who has compiled the book entitled **"Solid Waste Pollution and Health"** which is right time to introduce a book on this burning topic of environmental pollution.

I feel pleasure and honour to write the foreword of this book entitled **"Solid Waste Pollution and Health"**, compiled by **Professor Dr. E.H. El-Mossalamy.** The book is upto the mark, both in respect of its contents and literary presentation. The book is equally useful for students, young researchers and teachers. I am pleased to contribute for this book. Some of the current research material on this burning topic from Oriental Journal of Chemistry, Bhopal, India.

Dr. Syed Aftab Iqbal
Chief Editor
Oriental Journal of Chemistry
Bhopal, 462 001 (India)

CONTENTS

1 Introduction

There has been a continuous migration of people from rural and semi-urban areas to towns and cities. The proportion of population residing in urban areas has increased from 10.84 per cent in 1901 to 25.70 per cent in 1991. The number of class I cities has increased from 212 to 300 during 1981 to 1991 while class II cities have increased from 270 to 345 during the same period. The increase in the population in class I cities is very high as compared to that in class II cities, the uncontrolled growth in urban areas has left many deficient in infrastructural services such as water supply, sewerage and municipal solid waste management.

Most urban areas in the country are plagued by acute problems related to solid waste. Due to lack of serious efforts by town/city authorities, garbage and its management has become a tenacious problem and this not-withstanding the fact that the largest part of municipal expenditure is allotted to it. It is not uncommon to find 30-50 per cent of staff and resources being utilized by Urban Local Bodies for these operations. Despite this, there has been a progressive decline in the standard of services with respect to collection and disposal of municipal solid waste including hospital and industrial wastes, as well as measures for ensuring adequacy of environmental sanitation and public hygiene. In many cities nearly half of solid waste generated remains unattended, giving rise to insanitary conditions especially in densely polluted slums which in turn results in an increase in morbidity especially due to microbial and parasite infections and infestations, in all segments of population, with the urban slum dwellers and the warte handlers being the worst affected.

The collection and disposal of municipal solid waste is one of the pressing problems of city life which has assumed great importance in the recent past.

With the growing urbanization as a result of planned economic growth and industrialization, problems are becoming acute and calls for immediate and concerted action, the proper disposal of urban waste is not only absolutely necessary for the preservation and improvement of public health but it has immense potential for resource recovery. It is estimated that the total solid waste generated by 300 million people living in urban India is 38 million tonnes per year.

It is estimated that about 1,00,000 MT of municipal solid waste is generated daily in the country. Per capita waste generated in major cities ranges from 0.20 kg to 0.6 kg. The collection efficient ranges between 50 to 90 per cent of the solid waste generated leaving the balance unattended. It is also estimated that the Urban Local Bodies spend about Rs. 500 to Rs. 1,500 per ton on solid waste for collection, transportation, treatment and disposal. About 60-70 per cent of this amount is spent on collection, 20-30 per cent on transportation and less than 5 per cent on final disposal of waste, which shows that hardly any attention is given to scientific and safe disposal of waste, Landfill sites have not yet been identified by many municipalities and in several municipalities, the landfill sites have been exhausted and the respective local bodies do not have resources to acquire new land. Due to lack of disposal sites, even the collection efficiency gets affected.

Solid waste management is a part of public health and sanitation and according to the Indian Constitution, it falls within the preview of the State List, since this activity is non-exclusive, non-rivealed and essential, the responsibility for providing the service lies within the public domain, the activity being of a local nature, is entrusted to the Urban Local Bodies. The Urban Local Body undertakes the task of solid waste service delivery, with its own staff, equipment and funds. In a few cases, part of the said work is contracted to private enterprises.

There has been no major effort to build up informed community awareness either about the likely periods due to poor waste management or the simple steps that citizen can take which will help in reducing waste generation and promote effective management of solid waste generated. The degree of community sensitizations and public awareness is low. There is no system of segregation of organic, inorganic and recyclable wastes at household level, door to door collection is not practised in most of the cities.

Very few Urban Local Bodies in the country have prepared long-term plans for effective Solid Waste Management in their respective cities. For obtaining a long-term economic solution planning of the system on long-term sustainable basis is very essential.

Classification of Wastes

INTRODUCTION

Depending upon *the nature and characteristics of the waste*, the solid wastes are distinguished into various classifications. Solid waste in urban settings can be divided into two broad categories, namely (1) MSW (municipal solid wastes) and (2) ISW (industrial solid wastes).

Depending on their source solid waste can be classified into different types:

1. Municipal waste;
2. Industrial waste;
3. Hospital waste or biomedical waste; and
4. Hazardous waste.

MUNICIPAL SOLID WASTE

Municipal solid waste consists of household waste, construction and demolition debris, sanitation residue, and waste from streets. This garbage is generated mainly from residential and commercial complexes. Municipal solid wastes are collected and disposed off by municipal corporations and the industrial solid wastes are disposed by the respective industries.

Municipal solid waste (MSW) refers to those solid waste whose collection and disposal come under duly of the municipality or other local civic authorities. The proportions of different constituents of waste vary from season to season and place to place, depending on the lifestyle, food habits, standard of living, the extent of industrial and commercial activities in the area, and so on.

Composition of Municipal Solid Waste

MSW mainly includes the residential waste, abattoir waste, market waste, institutional waste, hospital waste, waste from schools, waste from hotels and restaurants, natural waste and waste during street sweeping.

All above compositions are described as under:

(a) ***Residential waste or garbage:*** The waste that is generated daily in residential areas comprises this category. Generally, it is known as 'Garbage' and this garbage includes rotten vegetables/fruits, kitchen waste, plastic glass etc.

(b) ***Abattoir waste:*** Delhi has at least 20 markets where illegal roadside slaughtering of sheep, goat, pigs etc. takes place. The conditions in these places are worse than those in Idgahs.

(c) ***Waste from hotels and restaurants:*** About 95 per cent of the waste generated from these places includes food items which is bio degradable the rest five per cent includes the packing materials such as boxes, papers, polythenes.

(d) ***Market waste:*** Of the total waste generated in Delhi, everyday markets produce approx. 26 per cent (2040 tonnes). Of this the biodegradable is 50 per cent and 27 per cent of which constitute recyclable type. The wholesale markets selling grains produce the wastes such as dead insects, rats etc. The shop keepers clean their shops and dump the wastes on roadside.

(e) ***Institutional waste and waste from schools:*** The main wastes from the institutions and schools include paper, cardboards, and left overs. This also contributes greatly towards the Municipal waste.

(f) ***Natural waste and waste during street sweeping:*** As the name indicates this is the type of waste which is absolutely natural and contributes 0.5 per cent of the Municipal waste.

(g) ***Hospital waste:*** Delhi has 27 major hospitals, thousands of nursing homes, dispensaries and veterinary hospitals, all of which are combined are responsible for generating 550 tonnes of the waste everyday. On an average, only 5-6 per cent of this is recyclable. Ragpickers pick only 1-2 per cent of it. The hospital waste include the items like saturated blood, body fluid, cotton, plaster etc. and infectious items, *e.g.* amputated, body-parts, cultures of contagious viruses, excreta from patients with highly contagious diseases, scalpels, needles, bandages, etc. from OTs and laboratories. Of the total waste produced in hospitals is 47.2 per cent is contaminated with pathogens, making it a hazardous biomedical waste.

Table 2.1 : The Data Collected on Quantity and Nature of Solid Waste (during 1996)

Sl. No.	Type	Quantity (tonnes/day)	Bio-degradable (%)	Recyclable (%)	Picked by ragpickers(%)
1.	Residential	3560 (42.1%)	60	35	40
2.	Market	2040 (25.8%)	50	27	80
3.	Hospital	550 (6.9%)	–	6	1–2
4.	Hotels	550 (6.9%)	50	40	10

INDUSTRIAL SOLID WASTE

Industries can be broadly classified into those that produce **non-hazardous waste** and those that produce hazardous waste. Reliable data on the quantity of solid wastes generated by small-scale industries are scarce. As small-scale industries have mushroomed everywhere, it is assumed that they generate as much industrial waste as that generated by medium and large-sized industries.

Table 2.2 : Annual Generation of Industrial Solid Waste

(in Million Tonnes)

Solid waste	Quantity
Fly ash	45.0
Slag	8.5
Phosphogypsum	5.0
Lime sludge	4.0
Red mud	3.5

Non-hazardous Wastes

Non-hazardous wastes can be either biodegradable or non-biodegradable:

(a) ***Biodegradable:*** The major industries in urban areas that generate substantial amounts of biodegradable solid waste are fruit processing, cotton mills, paper mills, sugar mills.

(b) ***Non-biodegradable waste:*** Non-hazardous non-biodegradable waste is commonly known as industrial solid waste. The major generators of non-biodegradable industrial solid waste are thermal power plants, which produce coal ash, integrated iron and steel mills, which produce blast furnace slag and steel melting slag, such non-ferrous industries as aluminum, zinc, and copper, which produce red mud and tailings and fertilizer and allied industries, which produce gypsum. Together, the industries generate huge amount of waste.

Hazardous Waste

Industrial and hospital waste is considered hazardous as it may contain toxic substances. Certain types of household waste are also hazardous. Hazardous wastes could be highly toxic to humans, animals, and plants; are corrosive, highly inflammable, or explosive, and react when exposed to certain things *e.g.* gases. India generates around seven million tonnes of hazardous wastes every year, most of which is concentrated in four States: Andhra Pradesh, Bihar, Uttar Pradesh, and Tamil Nadu. Some of the wastes generated by industries are deemed to be 'hazardous wastes' because they contain substances that are toxic to plants and animals or are flammable, corrosive, explosive, or highly reactive chemically. Hazardous waste presents, immediate or long-term risks to humans, animals, plants, or the environment. It requires special handling for detoxification or safe disposal (Table 2.3).

Table 2.3 : Types of Hazardous Waste

Regulatory category	Types of waste
No. 1.	Cyanide waste
No. 1 and 3	Metal finishing, waste containing mercury, arsenic, thallium, and cadmium.
No. 2	Waste containing water soluble chemical compounds of lead, copper, zinc,chromium, nickel, selenium, barium, and antimony.
No. 5 and 6	Waste containing non-halogenated and halogenated hydrocarbons including solvents.
No. 7 and 8	Wastes from dyes and dye-intermediates containing inorganic and organic chemical compounds.
No. 10, 11, 13	Waste oil and oil emulsions, phenols, tarry waste and residues from distillation or pyrolytic treatment
No. 12	FTP sludge containing heavy metals, toxic organic oil emulsions and spent chemical and incineration ash
No. 14	Asbestos
No. 15	Wastes from pesticides and herbicides (technical and formulating) units.
No. 16	Acidic or alkaline slurry
No. 17 and-18	Specified and discarded products/containers and container-liners of hazardous and toxic waste.

The major industries that produce hazardous wastes include metals, chemicals, drugs and pharmaceuticals, leather, pulp and paper, electroplating, refining, pesticides, dyes, rubber goods and so on. Table 2.4 shows the amount of wastes generated by such industries per unit output.

It is estimated that currently the industrial sector generates about 100 million tonnes of non-hazardous solid wastes and two million tonnes of hazardous waste a year.

Table 2.4 : Generation of Hazardous Waste from Select Industries/ industrial Products

(in Tonnes Per Tonne of Product)

Industry/Industrial product	Solid waste (*tonne/tonne of product*)
Caustic soda	0.03
Drugs and Pharmaceuticals	0.04
Dye and dye intermediates	1.36
Fertilizer	0.085
Inorganic chemicals	0.4
Organic chemicals	0.15
Pesticides	0.07
Petrochemicals	1.38
Refinery	0.015
Textile processing	0.02/1000m (2 grams/metre)

HOSPITAL/MEDICAL WASTE

Hospital wastes constitute an important category of solid waste. Hospital waste contaminated by chemicals used in hospitals is considered hazardous. These chemicals include formaldehyde and phenols, which are used as disinfectants, and mercury, which is used in thermometers or equipment that measure blood pressure. Most hospitals in India do not have proper disposal facilities for these hazardous wastes.

Hospital waste is generated during the diagnosis, treatment, or immunization of human beings or animals or in research activities in these fields or in the production or testing of biologicals. It may include wastes like sharps, soiled waste, disposables, anatomical waste, cultures, discarded medicines, chemical wastes, etc. These are in the form of disposable syringes, swabs, bandages, body fluids, human excreta, etc. This waste is highly infectious and can be a serious threat to human health if not managed in a scientific and discriminate manner. It has been roughly estimated that of the 4 kg of waste generated in a hospital at least one kg would be infected. Surveys carried out by various agencies show that the healthcare establishments in India are not giving due attention to their waste management. After the notification of the Bio-medical Waste (Handling and Management) Rules, 1998, these establishments are slowly 'streamlining the process of waste segregation, collection, treatment, and disposal'. Many of the larger hospitals have either installed the treatment facilities or are in the process of doing so. The proper management of hospital waste assumes greater significance in the context of the present times due to several reasons like an increase in the disease profile and the advent of several new antibiotics and drugs leading to a certain level of complacency on the part of the public, medical professionals and waste handlers alike. However, at many places, the public itself is becoming more aware about the hazards posed by hospital waste as well as by the traditional method of dealing with hospital waste-incineration.

Classification of Medical Wastes

Source segregation is imperative to the proper management of hospital wastes. To achieve this task, it is important to categorize the waste streams. The number and type of categories directly relate to the system that will eventually manage them. To make the system practically manageable, it is also important that the number of categories be kept to a minimum without sacrificing the efficacy and should be based on the specific mode of ultimate disposal of these categorized wastes.

The following broad classification of medical waste can be used for practical purposes:

1. Non-infectious wastes;
2. Infectious wastes and
3. Toxic wastes.

Non-infectious Wastes

This constitutes a major portion—nearly 90 per cent of the entire hospital waste generated. It is that part of the waste which is free from infection-spreading microbes and has not been in contact with any body fluids and is similar in nature to domestic waste.

Non-infectious waste is broadly classified into the following :

(*a*) General office waste, comprising wrapping paper, office paper, cartons, packaging materials like plastic sheets, newspapers, bouquets etc.

(*b*) Kitchen waste, including left-over food, swill, peels and dirty water generated from the hospital kitchen. Food wasted by those designated as infectious patients must be autoclaved before final disposal. The non-infectious waste generated from the kitchen can be biodegradabe or non-biodegradable.

Note : Gloves not contaminated with blood and with fingers cut and IV bottles can be classified as non-infectious.

Infectious Wastes

Potentially infectious wastes from patient care include :

(*a*) Dressing and swabs, contaminated with blood or body fluids;

(*b*) Laboratory waste including laboratory samples, culture stocks of infectious agents, laboratory glassware;

(c) Instruments used in patient care, these range from diagnostic equipment such as endoscopes, ultrasound probes, syringes and needles, sharps and other instruments, tubings and bags;

(d) Potentially infected materials, placenta, tissues, tumours, organs or limbs which are removed during surgery;

(e) Potentially infected animals - used in diagnostic or research studies.

In all these wastes, the major concern is to prevent potential accidental transmission of infection.

Toxic Wastes

Potentially toxic wastes are :

(a) **Radioactive waste :** These may be solids, liquids and gases used for analytical procedures, body organ imaging and tumour localisation and treatment.

(b) **Chemical waste :** These may be hazardous, toxic, corrosive, flammable, reactive or genotoxic.

(c) **Pharmaceutical agents :** These may enter hospital waste because there was surplus stock, spillage or contamination was detected or expiry dare was over. Potential health hazards may result from infectious and toxic hospital wastes.

The **W.H.O.** has categorized medical waste into eight groups, but for developing countries, a simplified classification has been recommended. This is as follows :

1. General hazardous wastes.
2. Sharps.
3. Chemical and pharmaceutical wastes.
4. Infectious wastes.
5. Other hazardous wastes.

PLASTICS

Plastic with its exclusive qualities of being light yet strong and economical, has invaded every aspect of our day-to-day life, it has many advantages: it is durable, light, easy to mould, and can be adapted to different user requirements. Once hailed as a 'wonder material', plastic is now a serious worldwide environmental and health concern, essentially due to its non-biodegradable nature.

In India, the plastic industry is growing phenomenally. Plastics have use in all sectors of the economy—infrastructure, construction, agriculture, consumer goods, telecommunications, and packaging. But the good news is that along with a growth in the use, a country-wide network for collection of plastic waste through rag pickers, waste collectors and waste dealers and recycling enterprises has sprung all over the country over the past decade or so. More than 50 per cent of the plastic waste generated in the country is recycled and used in the manufacture of various plastic products.

Conventional plastics have been associated with reproductive problems in both wildlife and humans. Studies have shown a decline in human sperm count and quality, genital abnormalities and a rise in the incidence of breast cancer. Dioxin a highly carcinogenic and toxic by-product of the manufacturing process of plastics, is one of the chemicals believed to be passed on through breast milk to the nursing infant. Burning of plastics, especially PVC releases this dioxin and also furan into the atmosphere. Thus, conventional plastics, right from their manufacture to their disposal are a major problem to the environment.

Plastic is so versatile in use that its impacts on the environment are extremely wide ranging. Careless disposal of plastic bags chokes drains, blocks the porosity of the soil and causes problems for groundwater recharge. Plastic disturbs the soil microbe activity, and once ingested, can kill animals. Plastic bags can also contaminate foodstuffs due to leaching of toxic dyes and transfer of pathogens. In fact, a major portion of the plastic bags *i.e.* approximately 60-80 per cent of the plastic waste generated in India is collected and segregated to be recycled.

The rest remains strewn on the ground, littered around in open drains, or in unmanaged garbage dumps. Though only a small percentage lies strewn it is this portion that is of concern as it causes extensive damage to the environment.

The plastic industry in the developed world has realized the need of environmentally acceptable modes for recycling plastics wastes and has set out targets and missions. Prominent among such missions are the Plastic Waste Management Institute in Japan, the European Centre for Plastics in

Source of generation of waste plastics	
HOUSEHOLD	Carry bags
	Bottles
	Containers
	Trash bags
HEALTH AND MEDICARE	Disposable syringes
	Glucose bottles
	Blood and uro bags
	Intravenous tubes
	Catheters
	Surgical gloves
HOTEL AND CATERING	Packaging items
	Mineral water bottles
	Plastic plates, glasses, spoons
AIR/RAIL TRAVEL	Mineral water bottles
	Plastic plates, glasses, spoons
	Plastic bags

Environment, the Plastic Waste Management Task Force in Malaysia. Manufacturers, civic authorities, environmentalists and the public have begun to acknowledge the need for plastics to conform to certain guidelines/ standards and code of conduct for its use.

Designing eco-friendly, biodegradable plastics is the need of the hour. Though partially biodegradable plastics have been developed and used, completely biodegradable plastics based on renewable starch rather than petrochemicals have only recently been developed and are in the early stages of commercialization.

3

Composition, Characteristics, Quantities and Environmental Effects

The information on the nature of wastes, its composition, physical and chemical characteristics and the quantities generated are basic needs for the planning of a Solid Waste Management System.

CLASSIFICATION OF SOLID WASTES

The solid waste can be classified based on source, origin and type of wastes:

(i) **Domestic/Residential waste :** This category of waste comprises the solid wastes that originate from single and multi-family household units. These wastes are generated as a consequence of household activities such as cooking, packaging, clothing, books and writing paper and old furnishings. Households also discard bulky wastes such as furniture and large appliances which cannot be repaired and used.

(ii) **Municipal Wastes :** Municipal wastes include resulting from municipal activities and services such as street, dead animals, market waste and abandoned vehicles. However, the term is commonly applied in a wider sense to incorporate domestic wastes, institutional wastes and commercial wastes

(iii) **Commercial Waste:** Included in this category are solid wastes that originate in offices, wholesale and retail stores, restaurants, hotels, markets, warehouses, and other commercial establishments. Some of these wastes are further classified as garbage and others as rubbish.

(iv) **Institutional Waste:** Institutional wastes are those arising from institutions such as schools, universities, hospitals and research institutes. It includes wastes which are considered to be hazardous to public health and to the environment.

(*v*) **Garbage:** Garbage is the term applied to animal and vegetable wastes resulting from the handling, storage, sale, preparation, cooking and serving of food since wastes contain prescribed organic matter, which produces strong odour and therefore attracts rats, flies and other vermin. It requires immediate attention in its storage, handling and disposal.

(*vi*) **Rubbish :** Rubbish is a general term applied to solid wastes originating in households, commercial establishments and institutions, including garbage and ashes.

(*vii*) **Ashes :** Ashes are the residues from the burning of wood, coal charcoal, coke and several other combustible materials, for cooking and heating in houses, institutions and small industrial establishments, when produced in large quantities at power generating plants and factories, these wastes are classified as industrial wastes. Ashes consist of a fine powdery residue, cinders and clinker often mixed with small pieces of metal and glass.

(*viii*) **Bulky Wastes :** In this category are bulky household wastes which cannot be accommodated in the normal storage containers of households. For this reason they require special collection. In developed countries bulky wastes are large household appliances such as cookers, refrigerators and washing machines as well as furniture, crates, vehicleparts, tyres, wood, trees and branches. Metallic bulky wastes are sold as scrap metal but some portion is disposed off at sanitary landfills.

(*ix*) **Street Sweeping :** This term applies to wastes collected from streets walk ways, alleys, parks and vacant plots. In the more affluent countries manual street sweeping has virtually disappeared but it still commonly takes place in developing countries where littering of public places is a for more widespread and acute problem. Mechanized street sweeping is the dominant practice in the developed countries. Street wastes include paper, cardboard, plastic, dirt, dust, leaves and other vegetable matter.

(*x*) **Dead Animals :** This is a term applied to dead animals that die naturally or accidentally killed. This category does not include carcasses and animals parts from slaughter-houses which are regarded as industrial wastes. Dead animals are divided into two groups - large and small. Among the large animals are horses, cows, goats, sheep, hogs and that like. Small animals include dogs, cats, rabbits and rats. The reason for this differentiation is that large animals require special equipment for lifting and handling during their removal. If not collected promptly dead animals are threat to public health because they attract flies and other vermin as they putrefy. Their presence in public places is particularly offensive and emits foul smell from the aesthetic point of view.

(*xi*) **Construction and Demolition Wastes :** Construction and demolition wastes are the waste materials generated by the construction, refurbishment, repair and demolition of houses, commercial buildings and other structures. It mainly consists of earth, stones, concrete, bricks, lumber, roofing materials, plumbing materials, heating system and electrical wires and parts of the general municipal waste stream, but when generated in large amounts at building and demolition sites, it is generally removed by contractors for filling low lying areas and by urban local bodies for disposal at landfills.

(*xii*) Industrial waste : In this category are the discarded solid materials of manufacturing processes and industrial operations. They cover a vast range of substances which are unique to each industry. For this reason they are considered separately from municipal wastes. It should be noted, however, that solid wastes from small industrial plants are frequently disposed of at municipal landfills.

(*xiii*) Hazardous wastes : Hazardous wastes may be defined as wastes of industrial, institutional or consumer origin which because of their physical chemical or biological characteristics are potentially dangerous to humans and the environment. In some cases although the active agents may be liquid or gaseous, they are classified as solid wastes because they are confined in solid containers. Typical examples are solvents, paints and pesticides, spent containers are frequently mixed with municipal wastes and become part of the urban waste stream. Certain hazardous wastes cause explosions in incinerators and fires at landfill sites. Others, such as pathological wastes, from hospitals and radioactive wastes require special handling at all time. Good management practice should ensure that hazardous wastes are stored, collected transported and disposed off separately, preferably after suitable treatment to render them innocuous.

(*xiv*) Sewage wastes: The solid by products of sewage treatment are classified as sewage wastes. They are mostly organic and derive from the treatment of organic sludge from both raw and treated sewage. The inorganic fraction of such as grit is separated at the preliminary stage of treatment because it entrains prescribed organic matter which may contain pathogens, must be buried off without delay. The bulk of treated, dewatered sludge is useful as a soil conditioner but invariably its use for this purpose is uneconomical. The solid sludge therefore enters the stream of municipal wastes unless special arrangements are made for its disposal.

The principal classification is given in Table 3.1. The first three types - garbage, rubbish and ashes - are those which make up the bulk of municipal wastes, derived particularly from household, institutions and commercial areas. Those wastes pose the most urgent problems in urban areas.

COMPOSITION AND CHARACTERISTICS

General

The composition and characteristics of municipal solid wastes vary throughout the world. Even in the same country it changes from place to place as it depends on number of factors such as social customs standard of living,

Table 3.1 : Classification of Solid Wastes

Types of Solid Waste	Description	Sources
Food waste (garbage)	Wastes from the preparation cooking and serving of food. Market refuse, waste from the handling, storage, and sale of produce and meats and vegetable.	
Rubbish	Combustible (primary organic) Paper, cardboard, cartons Wood, boxes, Plastics, Rags, cloth, bedding, Leather, rubber Grass, leaves, yard trimmings.	Households and commercial institutions such as hotels, stores; restaurants, marekets etc.
	Non-combustible (primary inorganic) Metals, tin cans, metal foils Dirt, Stones, bricks, ceramics, Crockery, Glass bottles, Other mineral refuse	
Ashes and Residues	Residue from fires used for cooking and for heating buildings, cinders, dinkers, thermal power plants.	
Bulky waste	Large auto parts, tyres, stoves refrigerators, other large appliances, furniture, large cities, trees branches, palm fronds, stumps, flouage.	
Street waste	Street sweepings, dirt, leaves, catch basin dirt, contents of litter receptacles Dead animals.	Streets, sidewalks, alleys, vacant lots, etc.
Dead animals	Small animals: cats, dogs, poultry etc. Large animals: horses, cows etc:	
Construction and demolition waste	Lumber, roofing and sheathing scraps, crop residues, ruble, broken concrete, plaster, conduit pipe, wire insulation etc.	Construction and Demolition sites Remodelling, Repairing sties
Industrial waste and sludges	Solid wastes, resulting from industry processes and manufacturing operations, such as food processing wastes, boiler house cinders, wood, plastic and metal scraps and shaving etc. ETP sludges of industries and sewage treatement plant sludges coarse screening, grit from septic tank.	Factories, power plants, treatment plants, etc.
Hazardous wastes	Hazardous wastes: pathological waste, explosives, radioactive material, toxic waste etc.	Households, hospitals, institution, stores industry etc.
Horticulture wastes	Tree-trimmings, leaves.	Parks, gardens, roadside trees, etc.,

Source: *Solid Waste Management in Developing Countries* by Bhide and Shunderasam, INSDOC April, 1983.

geographical location, climate etc. MSW is heterogeneous in nature and consists of a number of different materials derived from various types of activities. Even then it is worthwhile to make some general observation to obtain some useful conclusions:

- The major constituents are paper and putrescible organic matter.
- Metal, glass, ceramics, plastics, textiles, dirt and wood are generally present although not always so, the relative proportions depending on local factors.
- The average proportion of constituents reaching a disposal site(s) for a particular urban area changes in long term although there may be significant seasonal variations within a year.

For these reasons an analysis of the composition of solid wastes for rich and poor countries a like, is expressed in terms of a limited number of constituents. It is useful in illustrating the variations from one urban centre to another and from country to country. Dats for different degrees of national wealth (annual per capita income) are presented in Table 3.2, waste composition also varies with socio-economic status within a particular community. Since income determine life-style-composition patterns and cultural behaviour.

Table 3.2 : Patterns of Composition, Characteristics and Quantities

Composition (% by weight)	Low income countries (1)	Middle income countries (2)	High income countries (3)
Metal	0.2–2.5	1–5	3–13
Glass, Ceramics and food	0.5–3.5	1–10	4–10
Garden waste	40–65	20–60	20–50
Paper	1–10	15–40	15–40
Textiles	1–5	2–10	2–10
Plastic/Rubber	1–5	2–6	2–10
Misc. combustible	1–8	–	–
Misc. Incombustible	–	–	–
Inert	20–50	1–30	1–20
Density (kg.m^3)	250–500	170–330	100–170
Moisture content (% by wt.)	40–80	40–60	20–30
Waste generation (kg/cap/day)	0.4–0.6	0.5–0.9	0.7–1.8

Several conclusions may be drawn from this comparative data :

- The proportion of paper waste increase with increasing national income ?
- The proportion of putrescible, organic matter (food waste) is greaier in countries of low income than those of high income.
- Variation in waste composition is more dependent on national income than geographical location, although the latter is also significant.

- Waste density is a function of national income being two to three times higher in the low income countries than in countries of high income.
- Moisture content is also higher in low income countries.
- The composition of waste in a given urban centre varies significantly with socio-economic status (household income).

Characteristics of MSW in Indian Urban Centres

NEERI has carried out intensive characterization of solid waste from 43 cities during 1970-1994. The average characteristics based on study in 43 cities are given in Table 3.3 and Table 3.4. The paper content generally varies between 2.9 to 6.5 per cent and increases with the increase in population. The plastics,

Table 3.3 : Physical Characteristics of Municipal Solid Wastes in Indian Cities

Population Range (*in million*)	Number of cities surveyed	Paper	Rubber, Leather and Synthetics	Glass	Metal	Total Compostable Matter	Inert
0.1 to 0.5	12	2.91	0.78	0.56	0.33	44.57	43.59
0.5 to 1.0	15	2.95	0.73	0.35	0.32	40.04	48.38
1.0 to 2.0	9	4.71	0.71	0.46	0.49	38.95	44.73
2.0 to 5.0	3	3.18	0.48	0.48	0.59	56.67	49.07
> 5	4	6.43	0.28	0.94	0.80	30.84	53.90

Table 3.4 : Chemical Characteristics of Municipal Solid Waste in Indian Cities

Population range (*in million*)	No.of Cities surveyed	Moisture %	Organic matter %	Nitrogen as Total Nitrogen %	Phosphorous as P_2O_5 %	Potassium as K_2O %	C/N Ratio	Calorific Value in KCal/Kg
0.1–0.5	12	25.81	37.09	0.71	0.63	0.83	30.94	1009.89
0.5–1.0	15	19.52	25.14	0.66	0.56	0.69	21.13	900.61
1.0–2.0	9	26.96	26.89	0.64	0.82	0.72	23.68	980.06
2.0–5.0	3	21.03	25.60	0.56	0.69	0.78	22.45	907.18
>5.0	4	38.72	39.07	0.56	0.52	0.52	30.11	800.70

rubber and leather contents are lower than the paper content and do not exceed one per cent except in metropolitan cities. The metal content is also low, *viz.* less than one per cent. The low values are essentially due to the large scale recycling of these constituents. The paper is recycled on a priority basis while the plastics and glass are recycled to a lesser extent. The biodegradable fraction is quite high, essentially due to the habit of using fresh vegetables in India. The high biodegradable fraction also warrants frequent collection and removal of solid waste from the collection points. The ash and fine earth content of Indian MSW is high due to the practice of inclusion of the street sweepings, drain silt, and construction and demolition debris in MSW. The proportion of ash and fine earth reduces with increase in population due to improvement in the road surface. Percentage of inert material increases with the increase in population. To ash and earth content increases the densities of MSW which are between 350 and 550 kg/m^3 in Indian cities. The chemical characteristics indicate that the organic content of the samples on a dry weight basis ranges between 20 to 40 per cent. The Nitrogen, Phosphorous and Potassium (N.P.K.) content of the MSW ranges between 0.5 to 0.7 per cent, 05-0,8 per cent and 0.5 to 0.8 per cent respectively. The calorific value ranges between 800-1000 kcal/kg knowledge of the chemical characteristics is essential in selecting and designing the waste processing and disposal facilities.

Ragpickers are observed to be more active in bigger cities. They prefer to remove paper, plastics rags and packaging and such other material which is light and also has a high calorific value. The remaining waste hence tends to have a higher inert content and a lower calorific value.

The demolition activity is observed to increase with population leading to increased inert content and reduced organic content in MSW.

Composition

The composition of garbage in India, indicates lower organic matter and high ash or dust contents. It has been estimated that recyclable content in solid wastes varies from 13 to 30 per cent and compositible material is about 80-85 per cent.

A typical composition of MSW is given below in Table 3.5.

Table 3.5 : Composition of Municipal Solid Waste

Description	Per Cent by Weigth
Vegetables leaves	40.15
Grass	3.80
Paper	0.81
Plastic	0.62
Glass/Ceramics	0.44
Metal	0.64
Stones/Ashes	41.81
Miscellaneous	11.73

Quantities

The information regarding waste quantity and density coupled with waste generation role (by weight), is important while accessing the payload capacity of the collection equipment. It is possible to estimate the number of vehicles required for the collection and transportation of waste each day.

While per capita waste generation is a statistic which is necessary for indicating trends in consumption and production, the total weight and volume of wastes generated by the community served by the management system are of greater importance in planning and design. As in all other aspects of data collection for the planning and design phases, data on waste generation weight and volume should be collected by each authority for application in its own area of operation.

The quantity of waste from per capita quantity of MSW in Indian urban centres in various cities was accurately measured on the basis of quantity transported per trip and the number of trips made per day. The quantity of waste produced is lesser than that in developed countries and is normally observed to vary between 0.2-0.6 kg/capita/day value up to 0.6 kg/capita/day are observed in metropolitan cities (Table 3.6), the total waste generation in urban areas in the country is estimated to be around 38 million tonnes per annum.

Table 3.6 : Quantity of Municipal Solid Waste in Indian Urban Centres

Population range (*in million*)	Number of urban centres	Total population (*in milion*)	Average per capita value (*kg/capita/day*)	Quantity *tonnes/day*
< 0.1	328	68.300	0.21	14343
0.1–0.5	255	56.914	0.21	11952
0.5–1.0	31	21.729	0.25	5432
1.0–2.0	14	17.1784	0.27	4640
2.0–5.0	6	20.597	0.35	7209
> 5.0	3	26.307	0.50	13153

Forecasting waste quantities in the future is as difficult as it is in predicting changes of waste composition. The factors promoting change as waste composition are equally relevant to changes in waste generation. An additional point, worthy of note, is the change of density of the waste as the waste moves through the management system, from the source of generation to the point of ultimate disposal. Storage methods, salvaging activities, exposure to the weather, handling methods and decomposition, all have their effects on changes as waste density. As a general rule, the lower the level of economic development, the greater is the change between generation and disposal. Increases in density of 100 per cent are common in developing countries, which mean that the volume of wastes decreases by half.

Estimation of Future Per Capita Waste Quantity

For purposes of project identification, where an indication of service level must be estimated and data from the project preparation stage have not yet been developed. The following municipal refuse generation rates are suggested :

Residential refuse	0.3 to 0.6 kg/cap/day
Commercial refuse	0.1 to 0.2 kg/cap/day
Street sweeping	0.05 to 0.2 kg/cap/day
Institutional refuse	0.05 to 0.2 kg/cap/day

Table 3.7 : The Quantities of Municipal Solid Wastes Generation in Metro Cities

Sl.No.	City	MSW (TPD)	Per Caita Waste (*Kg/day*)
1.	Ahmedabad	1,683	0.585
2.	Bangalore	2,000	0.484
3.	Bhopal	546	0.514
4.	Mumbai	5,355	0.436
5.	Calcutta	3,692	0.383
6.	Coimbatore	350	0.429
7.	Delhi	4,000	0.475
8.	Hyderabad	1,566	0.382
9.	Indore	350	0.321
10.	Jaipur	580	0.398
11.	Kanpur	1,200	0.640
12.	Kochi	347	0.518
13.	Lucknow	1,010	0.623
14.	Ludhiana	400	0.584
15.	Chennai	3,124	0.657
16.	Madurai	370	0.392
17.	Nagpur	443	0.273
18.	Patna	330	0.360
19.	Pune	700	0.312
20.	Surat	900	0.600
21.	Vadodara	400	0.389
22.	Varanasi	412	0.400
23.	Visakhapatnam	300	0.400

Note: If industrial solid waste is included in municipal refuse for collection and/or disposal purpose, from 0.1 to 1.0 kg/cap/day may be added at the appropriate step where the municipality must estimate service delivery requirements. These generation rates are subject to considerable site specific factors and are required to be supported by field data.

Relation between Gross National Product (GNP) and MSW Generation

The consumption of raw materials and finished product by the community is directly proportional to the Gross National Product (GNP) of the country. Since the solid waste quantities are directly proportional to the quantity of material consumed the increase in per capita solid waste quantities would be directly proportional to the per capita increase in GNP.

Rate of Increase based on Experience in Other Cities

If data from other cities having registered similar pattern of development in the past is available, it can be used. However, data from other similar cities on rate of increase in per capita per day of solid waste may not be readily available. Due to difference in socio-economic factor, migration of population, industrialization and waste quantities, a comparison of increase in per capita waste of one Indian city with that of comparable cities in other developing countries will also not be applicable.

Seasonal Variations

Seasonal variations in waste quantities must be accommodated by the management system. They arise from seasonal factor with respect to both climate, cultural and religious events. During monsoon, the waste becomes wet and heavy and total tonnage increases. Quantities of solid waste may also increase during cultural and religious festivals. Climate effects the generation of vegetative waste (yard and garden) or plant growth responds to favourable temperatures and soil to autumn while in tropical areas, where temperature is always favourable maximum growth is in the season of rain fall. At the end of the growth season (autumn dry season) leaves may comprise a significant property of the solid wastes.

HEALTH AND ENVIRONMENTAL EFFECTS

Public Health

The World Health Organization has defined health is a state of complete physical, metal and social well-being and not merely the absence of disease or infirmity. This means that there are many dimensions to the problem of maintaining a healthy community. SWM is but one of them. Apart from its direct and indirect effects through accidents, exposure and the spread of disease one must also include the effects of visual pollution caused by litter and the nuisances created by smoke and dust at disposal sites.

Disease Vectors and Pathways

Solid wastes dumped indiscriminately provide the food and environment for thriving populations of vermin which are the agents of disease. The pathways of pathogen transmission from waste to humans are mostly indirect through insects - flies mosquitoes and roaches and animals - rodents, pigs. The discussion which follows considers the role of the most important of these vectors in the spread of disease. In general two conditions are necessary for diseases to become a public health problem:

- The disease must be present in the human and animal population of the surrounding communities;
- There must be a carrier to transmit the etiological agent from the last to the receptor.

Flies

The most important of the flies is the housefly which transmits over twenty diseases among which are—typhoid fever, Salmonellosis, Gastroentritis and

Dysentery. Flies have a flight range of about 10 km so they are able to spread their influence over a relatively wide area. There are few stages in their life cycle:

$$\text{Egg} \rightarrow \text{Larva} \rightarrow \text{Pupa and Adult}$$

Eggs are deposited in the warm moist environment of decomposing food wastes. When they hatch, the larva feed on the organic material until a certain maturity is reached, at which time they migrate from the waste to the soil or other dry loose material before being transformed into pupae. The pupae are inactive until the adult fly emerges. The migration of larvae within 4 to 30 days provides the due to an effective control measures, which is that the waste should be moved before migration occurs. Consequently, in warm weather, municipal waste should be collected twice weekly, at least for effective control. In addition the quality of household and commercial storage containers is very significant. The guiding principle here is restriction of access by flies to the stored waste. Clearly, the use of sound storage containers and general cleanliness at the sites of their location, as well as frequent collection of waste are measures which greatly reduce the population of flies. Control is also necessary at transfer stations, composting facilities and disposal sites to prevent them becoming breading ground for flies. Covering solid wastes with a layer to earth at landfill sites at the end of every day arrests the problem of fly breeding at the final stage of waste management.

Mosquitoes

Mosquitoes infect humans through attack by the female which transmits diseases like malaria fever, yellow fever and dengue fever since they breed in water, centre around the elimination of breeding places such as tin, cans and tyres that are so much a feature of open dumps. Proper sanitary landfill practices and general cleanliness in the community eliminate the mosquito problems caused by solid waste.

Roaches

Roaches cause infection by physical contact and can transmit typhoid fever, cholera and ameobiasis. The roach problem is associated with the poor storage of soil waste in house holds and commercial establishments. If containers are kept properly closed and inaccessible, the problem can be eliminated.

Rodents

Rodents, notably rats, proliferate in uncontrolled deposits of solid waste which provide or convenient source of food and shelter. They are responsible for the spread of 22 diseases including, marine typhus, leptospirosis, hostoplasmosis, rat bile fever, salmonellosis and trichonosis.

Many diseases are also caused by fleas which rats carry. The problem is not only on of open dumping but also of poor sanitation in surrounding households which are invaded only if they provide suitable breeding grounds and food supplies. A properly operated sanitary landfill should have no rats.

Accidents

Workers handling solid waste are at risk of accidents related to handling operations, the nature of material handling and the safty precautions employed. They suffer skin wounds by contact with the sharp edges of glass and metals and of poorly-constructed storage containers. It is good practice for waste handlers to wear gloves and to be vaccinated against tetanus.

Animals

Apart from rodents the pig is the most notable animal involved in the spread of diseases, especially in low income countries. Diseases the trichinosis, cryticerosis and toxoplasmosis are transmitted through infected pork eaten in an underdone or raw state when the animal is improperly fed raw solid waste.

Other Factors

- Muscular strain in collection workers as a result of the strenuous and augumentric physical effort of handling containers. These complaints are directly related to the weight of containers and the loading heights of vehicles, which should be limited to 20 kg and one metre respectively.
- *Dust a disposal sites:* This can cause lung and eye diseases as well as creating a nuisance protection against dust means the provision of suitable marks and airtight cabins for the use of workers, dust reduces visibility along access routes their creating greater risk of accident.
- Transmission of diseases by birds, vulture, harbours, the pathogen of toxoplasmosis.
- *Explosive hazards of solvents and fuels (garolom):* It is common practice to dispose of containers used for such liquids at landfill sites for municipal wastes, sufficient quantities of the contents may remain to create explosive mixtures
- Toxic chemicals used as pesticides, cleaning solutions and solvents in households and commercial establishments, although the quantities of these liquid resides are small they may be very toxic if ingested or absorbed through the skin.
- The careless dumping of lead acid, nickel-cadmium and mercuric oxide batteries serious health hazard, particularly for children, battery manufacturers can assist by providing collection services.

Environmental Effects

Air Pollution

1. Burning of solid wastes in open dumps or in improperly designed incinerators represents a significant source of air pollution and should be prohibited.

2. Effects of open burning were greater than incinerator especially in respect of aldehydes and particulates. Emissions from an uncontrolled incinerator system include particulates sulphur oxides, nitrogen oxides, hydrogen chloride, carbon monoxide, lead and mercury. Indeed all metals present in solid wastes can be discharged as particulates. Arsenic, cadmium and selenium are included in the list and since they are toxic at relative low exposure levels, their discharge should be controlled. A new poignant, dioxin, which is one or two general classes of organic compounds that are of concern because of their toxicity, carcinogenecity and possibly mutagenicity. These classes are: Polychlorinated dibenzofurans (PCDF's) commonly called dioxin and furans. The establishment of standards for the emissions from solid waste incineration systems is still in the evolutionary stage as new analytical techniques are developed for detecting a greater number of compounds of high toxicity.

Water and Land Pollution

1. Water pollution results from open dumping and the improper design, construction and/or operation of a sanitary landfill.
2. Control of infiltration from rain fall and surface runoff is essential in order to minimize the production of ground water can occur in the following ways:
   - by direct horizontal contact when groundwater flows through deposits of solid waste;
   - Through the vertical flow of percolating water from rainfall or irrigation or from the solid wastes themselves down to the water-table;
   - Through the transfer, by diffusion and collection of gases generated by the decomposition of solid wastes.

The interaction between leachate contaminants and the soil depends on the characteristics of the soil. BOD is stabilized by soil bacteria if toxic substances are in low concentration by anaerobic action. The carbon dioxide produced keeps the level low causing the water to dissolve minerals in the aquifers. Consequently the change in groundwater quality may be significant depending on the characteristics of the aquifer. Increases in hardness and iron and manganese compounds are common contamination can spread over considerable distances from the landfill if the aquifers are of sand or graved. In clay soils the rate of movement is greatly reduced. The capacity of clays to exchange ions restricts the involvement of metal cons by capturing them in the soil.

Visual Pollution

The aesthetic sensibility of concerned citizens of all countries is offended by the unsightliness of piles of waste, in general disorder, that are to be found in both developed and developing countries. Chief among them eye sores is the open dump—which unfortunately has not yet been laid to rest. In both middle and low income countries, the situation is made worse by the presence of scavengers rummaging in the waste. While one must concede that such activities are difficult to eliminate in conditions of poverty and high unemployment, the more enterprising of low income countries have shown that salvaging of materials can be organized at sanitary landfills by providing relatively simple and inexpensive facilities, such as a portable conveyor belt, for sorting and separation of waste components.

Other examples are waste carelessly irresponsibly discarded in public thoroughfares, along roads and highways and around communal bins, make shift containers, without lids used for the storage of residential commercial and institutional wastes, giving easy access to animals scavenging for food waste deliberately thrown into open drains. In some cases, the solid waste management authority is culpable by not providing containers in sufficient number, but there is little doubt that the irresponsible attitude of certain members of the public is at the heart of the problem. The solution of this social problem undoubtly lies in the implementation of vigorous programmers of public education at all levels primary, secondary, tertiary and adult, both short-term and long term, and in raising the status of workers and managers in the solid waste industry.

Noise Pollution

Undesirable noise is a nuisance associated with operations at landfills at sites of incinerators at transfer stations and at sites used for recycling. This is due to the movements of vehicles, the operation of large machines and the diverse operation at an incinerator site. The impacts of noise pollution may be reduced by careful siting of SWM operations and by use of noise barriers.

Odour Pollution

Foul odours are a feature of open dumps because of the presence of decaying organic matter. They arise from anaerobic decomposition processes some of waste products are particularly offensive. Proper landfill covering eliminated this nuisance.

Source Activities Generate Municipal Solid Waste

Explosion Hazard

1. Landfill gas which is released in anaerobic decompositon processes contains a high proportion of methane (35-73%) and is therefore potential explosive
2. It can migrate through the soil over a considerable distance, so that buildings in the vicinity of sanitary landfill sites are at risk even after their closure.

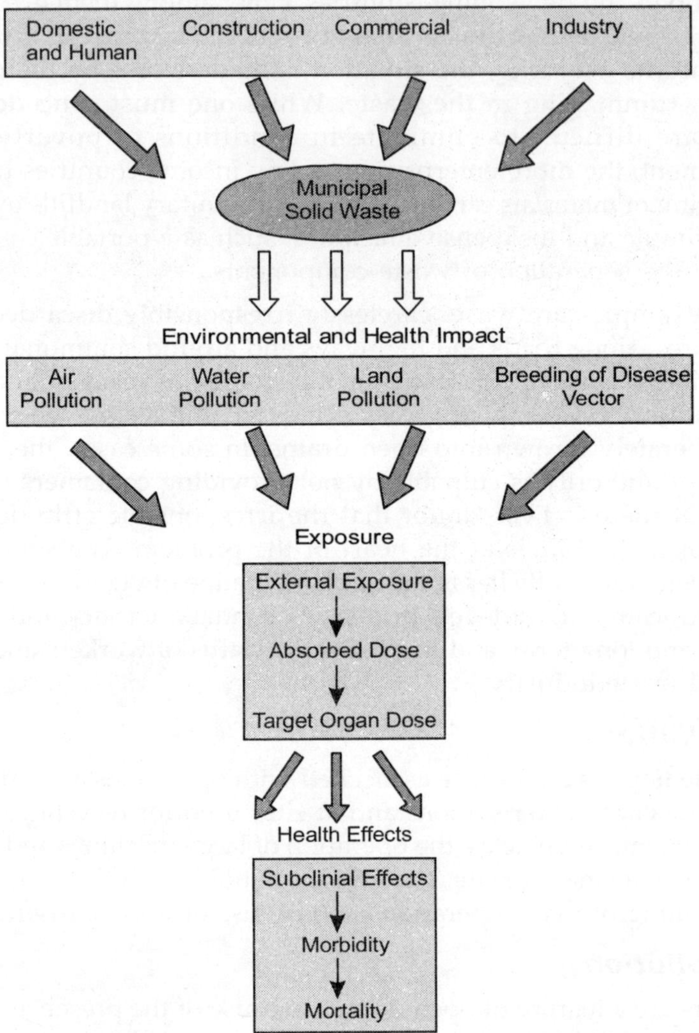

Fig. 3.1 Flowsheet of Environment and Health Impact of Municipal Solid Waste

3. Several methods are available for control of landfill gas, such as venting, flaming and the use of impermeable barriers.

Waste Storage, Collection and Transportation

CONSTRUCTION AND DEMOLITION WASTE

Construction and demolition waste is generated whenever any construction/ demolition activity takes place, such as building, roads, bridges, flyover, subway, remodelling etc. It consists mostly of inert and non-biodegradable material such as concrete plaster, metal wood plastics etc. A part of this waste comes to the municipal stream.

These wastes are heavy having high density, often bulky and occupy considerable storage space either on the road or communal waste bin/ container. It is not uncommon to see huge piles of such waste, which is heavy as well, stacked on roads especially in large projects, resulting in traffic congestion and disruption. Waste from small generators like individual house construction or demolition, find its way into the nearby municipal bin/vat waste storage depots, makmg the municipal waste heavy and degrading its quality for further treatment like composting or energy recovery often it finds its way into surface drains, chocking them. It constitutes about 10-20 per cent of the MSW (excluding large construction projects)

Storage

These wastes are best stored at source, *i.e.* at the point of generation. If they are scattered or thrown on the road, they not only cause obstruction to traffic but also add to the workload of the local body. All attempts should be made to stick to the following measures:

- All construction/demolition waste should be stored with in the site itself. A proper screen should be provided so that the waste does not get scattered and does not become an eye sore.

- Attempts should be made to keep the waste segregated into different heaps as far as possible so that their further gradation and reuse is facilitated.
- Material, which can be reused at the same site for the purpose of construction, levelling, making road/pavement etc. should also be kept in separate heaps from those, which are to be sold or land filled.
- The local body or a private company may arrange to provide appropriate number of skip containers/trolleys on hire which may be parked at the site and removed with skip lifters or tractors as the case may be.
- Whenever a new streamlined system is introduced in a municipality the local body may consider using its old vehicles, especially, tractors and trailers or old lorries or tippers for this purpose.
- For large projects involving construction of bridges flyovers, subways etc. provision should be made or storage of waste material. Depending on the storage capacity, movement of the waste has to be planned accordingly. Otherwise, it would be result in job constraint as well as traffic bottlenecks.
- This subject is often neglected in case of repair/maintenance of roads, water pipes, underground telephone and electric cables etc. It is not uncommon to see that after such work, the waste remains piled for months on the roads or paramount. The concerned departments and contactors must co-ordinate with the municipality for removal of the debris generated. The municipality while giving permission for such work should clearly sort out the issue of removal of the debris and should insist that immediately after the job is over the road should be repaired and brought back to its normal shape.

Collection and Transportation

If the construction debris is stored in skips, then skip lifters fitted with hydraulic hoist system should be used for efficient and prompt removal. In case, trailer are used, then tractors may remove these. For handling very large volumes, front-end loaders in combination with sturdy tipper trucks may be used so that the time taken for loading and unloading is kept to the minimum.

For small generators of construction debris, *e.g.* petty repair/maintenance job there may be two options: (1) specific places for such dumping by the local body; and (2) removal on payment basis.

In case of small towns where skips and tipping trailers are not available, manual loading and unloading should be done.

INDUSTRIAL SOLID WASTE

Environmental pollution is the major problem associated with rapid industrialization, urbanization and rise in living standards of people. For developing countries, industrialization was must and still this activity very much demands to build self reliant and in uplifting nations economy. However, industrialization on the other hand has also caused serious problems relating to environmental pollution. Therefore wastes seem to be a by-product of growth. The country like India can ill-afford to lose them as sheer waste. On the other hand, with increasing demand for raw materials for industrial production, the non-renewable resources are dwindling day by day. Therefore, efforts are to be made for controlling pollution arising out of the disposal of wastes by conversion of these unwanted wastes into utilizable raw materials for various beneficial uses. The problems related to disposal of industrial solid waste are associated with lack of infrastructural facilities and negligence of industries to take proper safeguards. The large and medium industries located in identified (conforming) industrial areas still have some arrangement to dispose solid waste. However, the problem persist with small scale industries. In number of cities and towns, small scale industries find it easy to dispose waste here and there and it makes difficult for local bodies to collect such waste though it is not their responsibility. In some cities, industrial, residential and commercial areas are mixed and thus all waste gets intermingled.

Storage

The storage of industrial solid waste is often on of the most neglected areas of operation of a firm. Very little attention is paid to proper storage and heaps of mixed wastes piled against a wall or on open ground are a common sight in many factories Concrete bays or disused drums are also often used for storage. Sludges originating from holding tanks or interceptors do not present storage problems no separate sludge storage is required, because the sludge is retained in the tank until sufficient quantities are collected.

Waste is rarely covered, protected from vermin or protected in any manner. There are no restrictions on access and employees are often encouraged to sort through the waste and take away any useful material or articles they find. Waste is regarded as an unwanted product by firms and very often no senior person is assigned for its control.

Collection and Transportation

Manual handling of industrial waste is the usual practice in developing countries. There are very few mechanical aids for waste management. Wastes are shoveled by hand into storage containers and loaded manually into lorries, The people undertaking salvaging do so mainly by hand, picking out useful items, usually not even wearing gloves. Although there may not be a health risk in handling clean waste paper, people handling or salvaging waste without protective clothing are at risk when waste is nixed with chemicals. Apart from the likelihood of cuts caused by broken glass or sharp metals. Sorting through waste contaminated with hazardous chemical materials could cause skin burns, excessive lacrimation, or even loss of consciousness; chronic hazards include respiratory problems from dust inhalation and potential carcinogenicity from toxic chemicals present in discarded containers or surface deposits in other waste. Personnel handling waste from tanneries or hide processors may also be exposed to such diseases as anthrax. These precautions will reduce and minimize hazards associated with manual handling of industrial wastes. Personnel handling hazardous wastes should wear appropriate protective clothing. Mechanical methods for handling waste should be adopted wherever possible and people should be educated about the dangers of manual handling of hazardous waste.

Transportation of industrial waste in metropolitan areas of developing countries is generally not by purpose built vehicles such as skip carrying lorries, put by open trucks. The wastes are not covered during transportation. It is typical or firm not to have any standing arrangements with one contractor, but to allow collection by who ever is the contractor quoting lowest rates. It is rare for special arrangements to be mads for hazardous wastes; they are usually collected other wastes. Contractors who carry hazardous waste do no need to be censed and consequently. There is little control over either the types of firms engaged in carrying hazardous waste or the vehicles used. Drivers are not given a list of precautions to be taken there is no manifest or labelling system of wastes during transportation. Fly-tipping is often prevalent and wastes are often taken to disposal sites inappropriate for the type of waste concerned.

Bio-medical Waste

Medical care is vital for our life health and well-being. But the waste generated from medical activities can be hazardous, toxic and even lethal because of their high potential for diseases transmission. The hazardous and toxic parts of waste from health care establishments comprising infectious, bio-medical and radio-active material as well as sharps (hypodermic needles knives, scalpels etc.) constitute a grave risk. These are not properly treated/disposed or are allowed to get mixed with other municipal waste. It's propensity to encourage growth of various pathogen and vectors and its ability to contaminate other non hazardous/non-toxic municipal waste jeopardizes the efforts undertaken for overall municipal waste management. The rag pickers and waste workers are often worst affected because unknowingly or unwittingly, they rummage through all kinds of poisonous material while trying to salvage items which they can sell and for reuse. At the same time, this kind of illegal and unethical reuse can be extremely dangerous and even fatal. Diseases like cholera, plague, tuberculosis, hepatitis (especially, HBV), AIDS (HIV), Diphtheria etc. in either epidemic or even endemic form pose grave public health risks unfortunately, in the absence of reliable and extensive data, it is difficult to quantify the dimension of the problem or even the extent and variety of the risk involved.

Storage

Storage of waste is necessary at two points :

1. At the point of generation and
2. Common storage for the total waste inside or health care organization.

For small units, however, the common storage area may not be possible. Systematic segregated storage is the most important step in the waste control programme of the health care establishment. For ease of identification and handling it is necessary to use colour coding, *i.e.* use of specific coloured container with liner/scaled container (for sharps) for particular wastes. It must be remembered that according to the rules untreated waste should not be stored beyond a period of 48 hours.

(i) **Recommended Labelling and Colour Coding :** A simple and clear notice describing which waste should go to which container and how frequently it has to be routinely removed end to where is to be posted on the wall or a conspicuous place nearest to the container. The notice should be in Hnglish, Hindi and the predominant local language. Preferably, it should have drawing correlating the container in appropriate colour with the kind of waste it should contain.

(ii) **Segregated Storage in Separate Containers (at the point of generation):** Each category of waste has to be kept segregated in proper container or bag as the case may be such container bag should have the following property :

- It must be sturdy enough to contain the designed maximum volume and weight of the waste without any damage.
- It should be without any puncture/leakage.
- The container should have a cover preferably operated by foot. If plastic bags are to be used, they have to be securely fitted with in a container in such manner that they stay in place suring opening and closing of the lid and can also be removed without difficulty.
- The sharps must be stored in puncture proof sharps containers. But before putting them in the containers, they must be mutilated by a needle cutter, placed in the department/ward itself.

The Bags/Containers Should not be Filled More than 3/4th Capacity. Attempts should be made to designate fixed places for each container so that it becomes a part of regular scenario and part of regular scenario and practice for the concerned medical as well as nursing staff.

(iii) **Certification:** When a bag or container is sealed, appropriate label(s) clearly indicating the following information has to be attached. A water proof marker pen should be used for writing.

They should be labelled with the 'Biohazard' or 'cyto-toxic' symbol as the case may be according to the rules.

- The containers should bear the name of the department/laboratory from there the waste has been generated so that in case of a problem or accident, the mature of the waste can be traced back quickly are correctly for proper remediation and if necessary the responsibility can be fixed.
- The containers should also be labeled with the dates name and signature of the person responsible. This would generate greater accountability.
- The label should contain the name, address, phone/fax nos. of the sender as well as the receiver.
- It should also contain name, address and phone/fax nos. of the person who is to be contacted in case of any emergency.

(*iv*) **Common/Intermediate Storage area:** Collection room(s)/intermediate storage area where the waste packets/bags are collected before they are finally taken/transported to the treatment/disposal site are necessary for large hospitals having a number of departments, laboratories, OTs wards etc. This is ail the more important when the waste is to be taken outside the premises. Two rooms-one for the general and the other for the hazardous waste are preferable In case of shortage of rooms, the general waste (non-hazardous) can be directly stored outside in dumper containers with lids of suitable size. Arrangement for separate receptacles in the storage area with prominent display of colour code on the wall nearest to the receptacles has to be made, when waste carrying carts/containers arrive at this area, they have to be systematically put in the rebvant receptacle designated area.

(*v*) **Parking Lot for Collection Vehicles:** A shed with fencing should be provided for the carts, trolleys, covered vehicles etc. used for collecting or removing the waste material. Care has to be taken to provide separate sheds for the hazardous and non-hazardous waste so that there is no chance of cross contamination. Both the sheds should have a wash area provided with adequate water jets, drains, raised platform, protection walls to contain splash of water and proper drainage system.

Collection and Transportation

This activity has three components (*i*) collection of different kinds of waste and from waste storage bags/containers inside the hospital, (*ii*) transportation and intermediate storage of segregate waste inside the premises and (*iii*) transportation of the waste outside the premises (to the treatment/disposal facility).

(*a*) **Collection of waste inside the hospital/health care establishment:** The collection containers for bio-medical waste have to be sturdy, leak proof of adequate size and wheeled. Two wheeled bins of 120-330 litre capacity and four wheeled bins of 500-1000 litre capacity may be used. The four wheeled containers have two fixed wheels and two castors and they are fitted with wheel locking devices to prevent unwanted rolling. There should be no sharp edges or corners, especially in metallic bins.

For convenience as well as for avoiding any confusion, the colour code applicable for the bags/containers should also be used for the bins. Collection timings and duty chart should be put in a prominent place with copies given to al! the concerned waste collectors and supervisors. For general waste from the office, kitchen, garden etc. normal wheel barrows may be used.

(*b*) **Transportation of Segregated waste inside the premises:** All attempts should be made to provide separate service corridors for takina waste matter from the storage area to the collection room. Preferably these corridors should not cross the paths used by patients and visitors. The waste has to be taken to the common storage area first, from where it is to be taken to the treatment/disposal facility either within or outside the premises as the case may be.

The wheel-barrows containing general waste may be sent to a dumper container or further segregated.

(*c*) **Collection and transportation of waste for small units:** Smaller units, such as nursing homes, pathological laboratories etc. do not have many departments/divisions, the generation of waste is small and normally they do not have treatment facility for the bio-medical waste.

In their case, intermediate storage area is not required. They should install a needle cutter and a small device for cutting plastic tubing, gloves etc. In case of highly infectious bio-medical waste is expected to be generated, they may consider to install a separate steam autoclave of suitable size exclusively for this purpose. Adequate precaution must be taken toward if any occupational hazard or environmental problem. This particular autoclave should never be used for sterilizing medical supplies or repeal equipments such establishments require provision for segregated storage (according to the rules) which can be packed in sealed containers/sturdy bags and handed over to the agency carrying them to the common treatment/disposal facility.

(*d*) **Transportation of Waste Outside:** In case of off-site treatment, the waste has to be transported to the treatment/disposal facility site in a safe manner. The vehicle, which may be specially designed van, should have the following specification:

- It should be covered and secured against accident opening of door, leakage spillage etc.;
- The interior of the container should be lined with smooth finish of aluminums or stainless steel, without sharp edges/corners or dead spaces, which can be conveniently washed and disinfected;
- There should be adequate arrangement for drainage and collection of any run off/leachate, which may accidentally come

out of the waste bags/containers the floor should have suitable gradient, flow trap and collection container;

- The size of the van would depend on to the waste to be carried per trip;
- In case, the waste quantity per trip is small, covered container of 1-2 m^3 mounted on 3 wheeled chassis and fitted with a tipping arrangement can be used.

Environmental Concern

The following are the main environmental concerns with respect to improper disposal of bio-medical waste management:

- Spread of infection and disease through vectors (fly, mosquito insects etc.) which effect the in house as well as surrounding population;
- Spread of infection through contact/injury among medical, non-medical personnel and sweepers/rag pickers, especially from the sharps (needles, blades etc.);
- Spread of infection through unauthorized recycling of disposable items such as hypodermic needles, tubes, blades bottles etc.;
- Reaction due to use of discarded medicines;
- Toxic emissions from defective/inefficient incinerator ash/residues.

DOMESTIC WASTE

Storage of waste at source is the first essential step of Solid Waste Management. Every household, shop and establishment generates solid waste on day-to-day basis. This waste should normally be stored at the source of waste generation till collected for its disposal. In India, such habit has not been formed and in absence of the system of storage of waste at source the waste is thrown on the streets, treating streets as receptacle of waste. If the citizens show such apathy and keep an throwing the waste on the streets and expect that the municipal sweepers should/would clean the city. The cities will never remain clean. Even if the local body makes on arrangement to remove all the waste disposal of by the citizens on the street on day-to-day basis the city will remain clean only for 2/3 hours and not beyond till the habit of throwing waste on the streets is not changed. There is, therefore, a need to educate the people to store the waste at source, discharge the waste as per the directions of the local body and effectively participate in the efforts of the local body to keep the cities clean.

Storage at Source and Storage Depots

(*a*) No storage at source-waste deposited on the streets: Generally number of bins for storage of domestic, trade or institutional waste are kept at source. A very few people keep personal bin for the storage of domestic, trade or institutional waste at source. The percentage of such people is in significant under the situation most of the domestic waste as well as waste from shops, offices and establishments including hospitals, nursing homes, hotels restaurants and construction waste etc. colonies on the streets or is disposed of unauthorized on public or private open plots or even discharged off waste on drains or water bodies nearby resulting in clogging the drains, pollution of water resources and unsanitary conditions in the urban areas.

(*b*) **Storage of waste, wherever done does not synchronize with primary collection system:** System of storage of waste at source, however practiced, by and large does not synchronize with the system of primary collection with the result the waste stored at home, shops and establishments in the domestic trade or institutional bins also finds its way on the street resulting in an unhygienic condition on the streets. Some of the types of the bins presently used are as under:

- Buckets.
- Plastic bins.
- Plastic bags.
- Metal bins with or without lids.

Most of the bins used are without lids. These are unsuitable for storage of food waste for 24 hours in the Indian condition as waste starts stinking very fast due to putrefaction.

Storage Depots

All the waste collected through primary collection system, from the household, shops and establishment has to be taken to the processing or disposal site which can either be done by taking. The waste to the processing or disposal site directly necessitating a large fleet of vehicles and manpower or cost effective system are designed to ensure that all the waste collected from the source of waste generation is temporarily stored at a common place called waste storage depots and then transported in bulk to the processing or disposal sites. Such temporary arrangement for storage of waste is popularly known as dust bin or *dhalavs*, etc. This facility has to be so designed that the system synchronizes with the system of primary collection as well as transportation of waste.

In India the system of providing waste storage depots is most inefficient, unhygienic and unscientific, posing a serious threat to the health and environment in most of the cities. Waste storage depots are of the following types:

(*i*) Open sites.
(*ii*) Cement-concrete-cylindrical bins.
(*iii*) Masonry bins.
(*iv*) Metal rings.
(*v*) *Dhalavas* etc.

At some places metallic containers are also placed. Deposition of waste at the open waste storage sites is most unscientific and unhygienic. The waste is just dumped at such sites from the wheel barrows/hand carts and waste remains littered at such sites till removed causing in sanitary conditions, foul smells, and environmental pollution besides giving unsightly appearance. This waste also necessitates multiple handling till it is finally disposed off.

Similar is the position of cylindrical and masonry bins where waste over throws outside the bin as they are designed and not user friendly. Sweepers do not put the waste in such bins and instead throw the waste outside the bin due to wrong design of the hand cart and inappropriate size of the bin. These bins necessitate mechanical as well as manual handling of contaminated waste.

Large concrete bins or *dhalavas* are constructed at some places for bulk storage of waste. These designs are also unsuitable as sanitation workers do not throw the waste inside them but throw the waste at the entrance blocking the passage. Waste is thus seen more outside the bin than inside it. Waste stored at such depots also necessitates multiple handling.

Collection

Primary collection system is necessary to ensure that waste stored at source is collected regularly and waste is not disposed of on the streets, drains, water bodies etc. This step has to synchronize well with the first step of storage of waste at source.

In India, the system of primary collection of waste is practically non-existent as the system of storage of waste at source is not yet developed.

Doorstep collection of waste from households, shops and establishments is insignificant and wherever doorstep collection system is introduced through private sweepers or departmentally, the system does not synchronize further with the facility of waste storage depots and transportation of waste. The waste so stored is deposited on the streets or on the ground outside the dustbin. Thus streets are generally treated as receptacle of waste and the primary collection of waste is done, by and large, through street sweeping.

An appropriate system of primary collection of waste is to be so designed by the urban local bodies that it synchronizes with storage of waste at source as well as waste storage depots facility ensuring that the waste once collected reaches the processing or disposal site through a containerized system.

Transportation

The transportation of the waste stored at the waste storage depots at regular intervals is essential to ensure that no garbage bins/containers over flow and waste is not seen littered on the streets. Hygienic conditions can be maintained in the city/town only if regular clearance of waste from temporary waste storage depots (bins) is ensured.

The transportation system has to be so designed that it is efficient, yet cost effective. The system should synchronize with the system of waste storage depot and should be easily maintainable in the town/city.

The Present Scenario

(*i*) **Inefficient, and unscientific manual loading of waste:** In most of the cities/towns there is no synchronization between waste storage depots and transportation of waste stored in open spaces is either loaded manually or/with the help of loaders in traditional trucks. Manual loading takes time and reduces the productivity of the vehicle and manpower deployed. Besides manual handling if waste poses a threat to the health of the sanitation workers as the waste is highly contaminated.

Loading through loading machines necessitates large quantities of waste collected in open. The loading operation is cheap but the loaders cannot clean waste storage depots fully besides loading machine damage the flooring and screen walls very often necessitating frequent repairs. If repairs are not carried out on time, the damaged flooring becomes a source of nuisance.

In the cities where *dhalavs* or large masonry bins are used waste is not regularly removed from inside of such structures and loaders cannot effectively function for removal of waste from the corners of such structures. This uncollected waste putrefies and emanates foul smell causing nuisance and in sanitary conditions.

(*ii*) **Irregular Transportation:** The cities and towns generally have limited fleet of vehicle and most of them are old necessitating frequent repairs with the result the transportation of waste does not take place regularly. The waste is generally seen lying in heaps or scattered at the open or unscientifically designed dust bins giving unsightly appearance besides cajsing nuisance and unhygienic conditions.

(*iii*) **Underutilization of Fleet of Vehicles:** Most of the vehicles are manually loaded and the lorries which can easily take 5 to 6 tonnes of solid waste on one trip, carry only on to three tones of waste as monitoring system does not exist. In several cities small vehicles and even bullock carts are taken directly to landfill sites at a long distance. This makes the transportation operation very inefficient an uneconomical.

(*iv*) **Open Trucks Cause Nuisance:** Open trucks loaded with garbage made through the city and they emanate foul smell and cause nuisance to the people. At places where cover material is arranged, covering of trucks is done half-heartedly and nuisance continues.

(*v*) **Non-Routing of Vehicles:** Transportation and work is by and large ill-designed. The waste storage depots are not cleared at regular intervals and more of less fire fighting operations are earned out by the local bodies. These sites are attended more on the basis of the complaints received or pressure brought on local staff rather than following a system of regular removal of waste from waste storage depots. The system of routing of the vehicles and the clearance of the bins on day to day basis thus generally breaks down.

(*vi*) **Transportation of Waste from Hotels, Restaurants, Hospitals, Construction sites etc.:** In many of the cities there is no separate system of collection and transportation of these wastes and waste from the above sites is not cleaned regularly.

5

Waste
Safe Disposal

The method invariably adopted for disposal of MSW is land-filling. A landfill is a disposal facility where solid wastes are placed and stored in a open soil. A landfill is called sanitary landfill when the waste is compacted in layers and covered by soil at the end of each day's operation in order to minimize the threats to human health and the environment.

SANITARY LANDFILLS

The purpose of landfilling is to busy or alter the wastes so that they are no longer environmental or public health hazard. Landfills are not homogeneous and are usually made up of cells in which a discrete volume of waste is kept isolated from adjacent waste cells by a suitable barrier. A barrier between cells commonly consists of a layer of natural soil (clay) which restricts downward or central escape of the waste constituents of leachate.

Landfilling relies on containment rather than treatment for control of wastes. Technologically, it is an unsophisticated disposal method. Yet properly executed, it is a safe and by for a cheaper method than incineration. Appropriate liners for protection of the groundwater from contaminated leachate, run-off control, leachate collection and treatment, monitoring wells and appropriate final cover design are integral components of an environmentally sound sanitary landfill.

LAND-FILLING OF MUNICIPAL SOLID WASTE

(*a*) Landfilling will be done for the following types of waste :

(*i*) Comingled waste (mixed waste) not found suitable for waste processing;

(*ii*) Pre-processing and post-processing rejects from waste processing sites;

(*iii*) Non-hazardous waste not being processed or recycled.

(*b*) Landfilling will usually not be done for the following waste streams in the municipal solid waste:

(*i*) Bio-waste/garden waste;

(*ii*) Dry recyclables.

(*c*) Landfilling of hazardous waste stream in the municipal waste will be done at a hazardous waste landfill site: such a site will be identified by the state government and is likely to be operated by industries of a district/state. If such a landfill is not available, municipal authorities will dispose the hazardous waste in a special hazardous waste cell in the MSW landfill.

(*d*) Landfilling of construction and demolition waste will be done in a separate landfill where the waste can be stored and mixed for future use in earthwork or road projects. If such a landfill site is not available, the waste will be stored in a special cell at a MSW landfill from where it can be mined for future use. Construction and demolition waste can be used as a daily cover at MSW landfills; however only minimum thickness of cover should be provided.

ESSENTIAL COMPONENTS

The seven essential components of a MSW landfill are:

(*i*) A linear system at the base and sides of the landfill which prevents migration of leachate of gas to the surrounding soil;

(*ii*) A leachate collection and control facility which collects and extracts leachate from within and from the base of the landfill and then treats the leachate;

(*iii*) A gas collection and control facility (optional for small landfills) which collects and extracts gas from within and from the top of the landfill and then treats it or uses it for energy recovery;

(*iv*) A final cover system at the top of the landfill which enhances surface drainage, prevents infiltrating water and supports surface vegetation;

(*v*) A surface water drainage system which collects and removes all surface run-off from the landfill site;

(*vi*) An environmental monitoring system which periodically collects and analysis air, surface water soil gas and groundwater samples around the landfill site;

(*vii*) A closure and post-closure plan which lists the steps that must be taken to close and secure a landfill site once the filling operation has been completed and the activities for long-term monitoring, operation and maintenance of the completed landfill.

Potential Environmental Emissions

The environmental aspects of an operating landfill are dominated by the nuisance imposed on the neighbourhood, wind-blown litter and dust, noise, odourous gases, birds, vermin and insects attracted by the waste, surface run-off and the psychological disturbance of the view to the landfilled waste gas and leachate problems also arise during the operation phase, demanding significant environmental controls :

- Wind-blown litter and dirt are continuous reminders of the ongoing land fill operation and a significant nuisance to the neighbourhood. By careful covering of the waste cells with soil, the problem may be reduced, but complete avoidance is impossible at the tipping front of the landfill. Spraying water on dirt roads and waste in dry periods in combination with fencing and movable screens ai the tipping front may minimize the problem.
- Noise is caused by traffic of waste collection vehicles, emptying of the vehicles and by the compactors and earth moving equipment. In some cases large gatherings of birds create a noise problem. The noise problem may be reduced by technical improvements of the equipment by surrounding the fill area with soil embankments and by limiting the working hours. Plantings may reduce the noise level, if they provide a tall and tight vegetation.
- Birds, vermin, insects and other animals are attracted to the landfill for feeding and breeding. Since many of these animals may act as disease transmitters, their presence may constitute a potential health problem. The aggressive and effective feeding patterns of seagulls right at the tip front make it very difficult to effectively reduce their presence at landfills.
- Surface run-off which bas been in contact with the landfilled waste may be a problem in areas with intense rainfall or snow melt. If not controlled, heavily polluted run-off may enter directly into creeks and streams. Careful design and maintenance of surface drains and ditches, together with a final soil cover on completed landfill sections, may eliminate this problem.
- Views are often important elements of the quality of residential and recreational areas. An operating landfill where equipment and waste are exposed, may psychologically affect the appreciation of an attractive area. This problem may be reduced by careful design of screening soil embankments, extensive plantings and rapid covering and revegetation of filled sections.
- Gas released from the waste, resulting from degradation of the waste or from volatilization of waste components, will migrate vertically out of the filled area or horizontally through porous soil layers into

the soil of adjacent fields. The problems associated with the gas are odourous, release of explosive/flammable methane, health aspects related to specific compounds and damage of the vegetation due to oxygen depletion of the root zone. Methane generation may start a few months after disposal of the waste may continue for several decades. The gas control measures which may be introduced are liners, soil covers, passive venting or active extraction of gas for use or treatment before discharge to the atmosphere.

- Polluted leachate from the waste appears shortly after disposal of the waste The leachate is likely to be heavily polluted and may cause extensive groundwater pollution and, through subsurface migration extensive pollution of streams. Liners, drainage collection, treatment of leachates and groundwater quality monitoring downstream of the landfill are necessary. Since the subsurface migration of groundwater and leachate may be slow, the consequences of improper leachate controls may not emerge until decades later.

At the completed landfill, the local nuisances are negligible. The environmental aspects related to gas and leachate still persist, however. If insufficiently covered, an additional environmental disadvantage may emerge at the site of the completed landfill vegetation and crops grown on the completed site may have been in contact through their roots with the waste material and may have become, contaminated. However, at properly completed landfills the risk of contaminated vegetation and wildife at the site is avoidable.

Minimizing Environmental Impacts

As can be discerned from the previous discussion, the environmental effects related to sanitary landfilling are varied, ranging from local nuisances which may be abated by a tidy operation of the site, to the potential contamination of regional groundwater resources by migrating leachate. While many of the environmental effects may be minimized by current technology, the long-term aspects of gas and leachate still raise questions about the appropriateness of the current technology. Significant developments in the concepts and technology of landfilling with a view to the long term effects are expected in the decades to come. Meanwhile, meeting today's needs for landfill capacity, acceptable environmental impacts of a sanitary landfill can be obtained only if proper attention is paid to the environmental aspects at all stages and phases of a landfill; site selection design, construction, operation and maintenance. The quality control measures required for ensuring a low level of impact on the environment from the landfill must be carefully documented.

Site Selection

The feasibility of land disposal of solid waste depends on factors such as the type, quantity and characteristics of the waste, laws and regulations, public perception and acceptance, and the soil and site characteristics. This section focuses on those characteristics that are important when selecting a site for land disposal options. The design and management of landlfills are site specific. The technical and economical feasibility will depend on the topography, soils, climate and hydrology of the site, on transport distances from the waste sources to the site and on current and projected land uses.

The process of site selection can be considered to have at least three major components:

1. **General evaluation:** problem definition and initial solution evaluation, this screens out site alternatives that clearly are not feasible;
2. **Detailed analysis of feasible options:** closely evaluates the site, soil and ground water characteristics, includes economic and political considerations and narrow site options;
3. **Final site selection and design:** involves detailed economic, technical and political evaluations of specific sites.

LANDFILL PLANNING AND DESIGN

Design Life

A landfill design life comprises of an active period and an 'closure and post-closure' period. The active period may typically range from 10 to 25 years depending on the availability of land area. The closure and post-closure period for which a landfill is monitored and maintained will be 25 years after the active period is completed.

Waste Volume and Landfill Capacity

The volume of waste to be placed in a landfill is computed for the active period of the landfill taking into account (*a*) the current generation of water per annum and (*b*) the anticipated increase in rate of waste generation on the basis of post records or population growth rate.

The required landfill capacity is significantly greater than the waste volume it accommodates. The actual capacity of the landfill depends upon the volume occupied by the liner system and the cover material (daily intermediate and final cover) as well as the compacted density of the waste. In addition, the amount of settlement a waste will undergo due to over-burden stress and due to biodegradation should also be taken into account.

The density of waste varies on account of large variations in waste composition, degree of compaction and state of decomposition. Densities may range as low as 0.40 t/cu.m. For planning purposes, a density of 0.85 1/cu.m may be adopted for biodegradable wastes with higher values (typically 1.1 t/cu.m) for inert wastes.

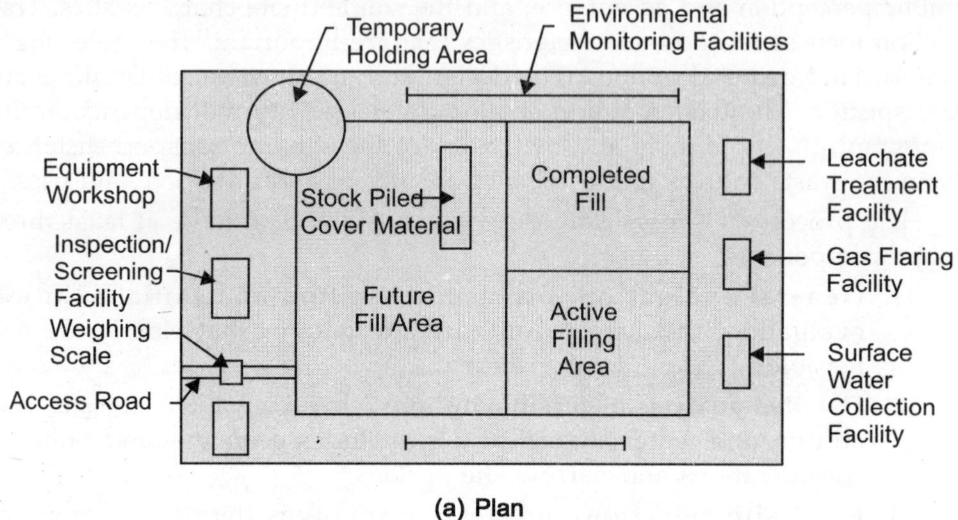

(a) Plan

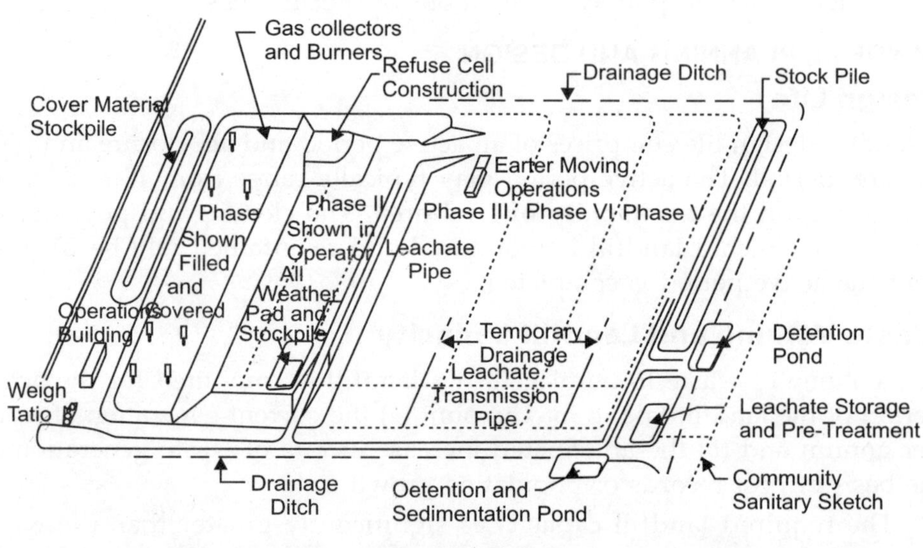

(b) Overview

Fig. 5.1 Typical Layout of a Landfill

Settlement of the completed waste mass beneath the final cover inevitably occurs as a result of the consolidation of waste within a landfill site. Initially settlement occurs predominantly because of the physical rearrangements of the waste material after, it is first placed in the landfill. Later settlement mainly results from biodegradation cf the waste, which in turn leads to further physical settlement. Accurate prediction of settlement is difficult because time related settlement data are readily rarely available. Initial settlement values of between 12 and 17 per cent have been reported for household waste sites in the U.K. with long-term (30 years values of approximately 20 per cent. A typical allowance of 10 per cent can be made when usable landfill capacity is computed (less than 5 per cent for incinerated/inert waste)

The total landfill area should be approximately 15 per cent more than the area required for landfilling to accommodate all infrastructure and support facilities as well as to allow the formation of a green belt around the landfill.

There is no standard method for classifying landfills by their capacity. However the following nomenclature is often observed in literature:

- Small size landfill: Less than 5 hectare area;
- Medium size landfill: 5 to 20 hectare area;
- Large size landfill: Greater than 20 hectare area.

Landfill heights are reported to vary from less than 5m to well above 30m.

Landfill Layout

A landfill site comprise of the area in which the waste will be filled as well as additional area for support facilities. Within the area to be filled, work may proceed in phases with only a part of the area under active operation. A typical site layout is already shown in Fig. 5.1(a). The following facilities must be located in the layout:

1. Access roads.
2. Equipment shelters.
3. Weighing scales.
4. Office space.
5. Location of waste inspection and transfer station (if used).
6. Temporary waste storage and or disposal sites for special wastes.
7. Areas to be used for waste processing (*e.g.* shredding).
8. Demarcation of the landfill areas and areas for stockpiling cover material and liner material.
9. Location of leachate treatment facilities.
10. Location of monitoring wells.

It is recommended that for each landfill site, a layout be designed in cooperating all the above mentioned facilities. The layout will be governed by the shape of the landfill area in plan.

Landfill Section

Landfills may have different types of sections depending on the topography of the area. The landfills may take the following forms:

(*a*) above ground landfills (area landfills);

(*b*) below ground landfill (trench landfills);

(*c*) slope landfills;

(*d*) valley landfills (canyon landfills); and

(*e*) a combination of Fig 5.1(b) shows typical landfill sections.

Above Ground Landfill (Area Landfill)

The area landfill (Fig 5.2 (*a*)) is used when the terrain is unsuitable for the excavation of trenches in which to place the solid waste. High-groundwater conditions necessitate the use of area type landfills. Site preparation includes the installation of a liner and leachate control system. Cover material must be hauled in by truck or earthmoving equipment from adjacent land or from borrow pit areas.

Below Ground Landfills (trench landfills) (Trench landfill)

The trench method of landfilling (fig 5.1 (*b*)) is ideally suited to areas where an adequate depth of cover material is available at the site and where the water-table is not near the surface. Typically, solid wastes are placed in trenches excavated from the site is used for daily and final cover. The excavated trenches are lined with low-permeability liners to limit the movement of both landfill gases and leachate. Trenches vary from 100 to 300m in length, 1 to 30 in depth, and 5 to 15m in width with side slopes of 2:1.

Slope Landfill

In hilly regions it is usually not possible to find that ground for land filling. Slope landfills and valley land fills have to be adopted. In a slope landfill waste is placed along the sides of existing hill slope. Control of inflowing wastes from hill side slopes is a critical factor in design of such landfills.

Valley Landfill

Depressions, low-lying areas, valleys, canyons, ravines, dry borrow pits etc. have been used for landfills. The techniques to place and compact solid wastes in such landfills vary with the geometry of the site the characteristics of the available cover material, the hydrology and geology of the site, the type of leachate and gas control facilities to be used, and the access to the site. Control of surface drainage is often a critical factor in the development of canyon/depression sites.

It is recommended that the landfill section be arrived at keeping in view the topography, depth to water table and availability of daily cover material.

Phased Operation

Before the main design of a landfill can be undertaken it is important to develop the operating methodology. A landfill is operated in phases because allows the progressive use of the landfill area, such that at any given time a part of the site may have a final cover a part being actively filled, a part being prepared to receive waste and a part undisturbed.

The term 'phase' describes a sub-area of the landfill. A 'phase' consists of cells, lifts daily cover, intermediate cover lines and leachate collection facility, gas control facility and final cover over the sub-area.

Each phase is typically designed for a period of 12 months. Phases are generally, filled from the base to the final intermediate cover and capped within this period leaving a temporary unrestored slopping face.

It is recommended that a 'phase plan' may be drawn as soon as the landfill layout and section are finalized. It must be ensured that each phase reaches the final cover level at the end of its construction period and that is capped before the onset of monsoons. For very deep or high landfills, successive phases should move from base to the top (rather than horizontally) to ensure early capping and less exposed plan area of 'active' landfills.

The term 'cell' is used to describe the volume of material placed in a landfill daring one operating period, usually one day. A cell includes the solid waste deposited and the daily cover material surrounding it. Daily cover usually consists of 15 to 30 cm of native soil that is applied to the working faces of the landfill at the end of each operating period. The purposes of daily cover are to control the blowing of waste materials, to prevent rate, flies and other disease vectors from entering or exiting the landfill and to control the entry of water into the landfill during operation.

A lift is a complete layer of cells over the active area of the landfill. Typically, each landfill phase is comprised of a series of lifts. Intermediate covers are placed at the end of each phase, these are thicker than daily covers, typically 45 cm or more and remain exposed tell the next phase is placed over it. A bench (or terrace) is commonly used where the height of the landfill will exceed 5 m. The final lift includes the cover layer.

The final cover layer is applied to the entire landfill surface oi the phase after all landfilling operations are complete. The final cover usually consists of multiple layers designed to enhance surface drainage, interrupt percolating water and support surface vegetation.

Estimation of Leachate Quality and Quantity

Leachate is generated on account of the infiltration of water into landfills and its percolation through waste as well as by the squeezing of the waste due to self weight. Thus, leachate can be defined as a liquid that is produced when water or another liquid comes in contact with solid waste. Leachate is a contaminated liquid that contains a number of dissolved and suspended materials.

Leachate Quality

The important factors which influence leachate quality include waste composition, elapsed time, temperature, moisture and available oxygen. In general, leachate quality of the same waste type may be different in landfills located in different climatic regions. Landfill operational practices also influence leachate quality.

Table 5.1 indicates the typical data on characteristics of leachate reported by Bagchi (1994), Tchobanoglous *et al.* (1993) and Oweis and Khera (1990).

Data on leachate quality has not been published in India. However, studies conducted by Indian Institute of Technology Delhi, NEERI, Nagpur and some State Pollution Control Boards have shown ground water contamination potential beneath sanitary landfills.

Table 5.1 : Typical Constituents of Leachate from MSW Landfills

Constitutent		Range (mg/l)	
Type	Parameter	Minimum	Maximum
Physical	pH	3.7	8.9
	Turbidity	30 JTU	500 JTU
	Conductivity	400 –mho/cm	72500 –mho/cm
Inorganic	Total Suspended Solids	2	170900
	Total Dissolved Solids	725	55000
	Chloride	2	11375
	Sulphate	0	1850
	Hardness	300	225000
	Alkalinity	0	20350
	Total Kjedahl Nitrogen	2	3320
	Sodium	2	6010
	Potassium	0	3200
	Calcium	3	3000
	Magensium	4	1500
	Lead	0	17.2
	Copper	0	9.0
	Arsenic	0	70.0
	Mercury	0	3.0
	Cyanide	0	6.0
Organic	COD	50	99000
	TOC	0	45000
	Acetone	170	11000
	Benzene	2	410
	Toluene	2	1600
	Chloroform	2	1300
	Delta	0	5
	1,2 dischlorethane	0	11000
	Methyl ethyl ketone	110	28000
	Nephthalene	4	19
	Phenol	10	28800
	Vinyl Chloride	0	100
Biological	BOD	0	195000
	Total Coliform bacteria	0	100
	Fecal coliform bacteria	0	10

Source: The above table is compiled from data reported by Bagchi (1994), Tchbanoglous *et. al.* (1993) and Oweis and Khera (1990). (It gives the range of constituents as observed in different landfills).

Assessment of leachate quality at an early stage may be undertaken to: (*a*) to identify whether the waste is hazardous; (*b*) to choose a landfill design; (*c*) todesign or gain access to a leachate treatment plant; and (*d*) to develop a list of chemicals for the groundwater monitoring programme. To access the leachate quality of a waste, the normal practice is to perform laboratory leachate tests (TCLP tests) as well as to determine the quality of actual landfill leachate, if available. Difficulty arises when field data are not available for a particular waste type Laboratory leachate tests on MSW do not yield very accurate results because of heterogeneity of the waste as well as difficulty as simulating of time dependent field conditions. Leachate samples from old landfill sites near the design site may give some indication regarding leachate quality; however this too will depend on the age of the landfill.

For the design of MSW landfills having significant biodegradable material as well as mixed waste, leachate quality has been universally observed to be harmful to ground quality. Hence, all landfills will be designed with a liner system at the base.

A landfill may not be provided a liner of and only if the following conditions can be satisfied:

(*a*) If the waste is predominantly construction material type inert waste without any undesirable mixed components (such as paints, varnish, polish etc.) and if laboratory tests (such as TCLP tests) conclusively prove that the leachate from such waste is within permissible limits; and

(*b*) If the waste has some biodegradable material, is must be proven through both laboratory studies on fresh waste and field studies (in old dumps) that the leachale from such waste will not impact the groundwater in all the phases of the landfill and has not impacted the groundwater or the subsoil so far in old dumps. Such a case may occur at sites where the base soil may be clay of permeability less than 10^{-7} cm/sec for at least 5m depth below the base and where water table is at least 20m below the base. A leachate collection facility would have to be provided in all such cases.

Leachate Quantity

The quantity of leachate generated us a landfill is strongly dependent on the quantity of infiltrating water. Thus, in turn, is dependent on weather and operational practices. The amount of rain falling on a landfill to a large extent controls the leachate quality generated. Precipitation depends on geographical location.

Singificant quantity of leachats is produced from the active phases of a landfill under operation during the monsoon season. The leachate quantity from those portions of a landfill which have received a final cover is minimal.

Generation Rate in Active Area

The leachate generation during the operational phase from an active area of a landfill may be estimated in a simplified manner as follows:

Leachate volume = (volume of preciptation)+(volume of pore squeeze liquid)–(volume lost through evaporation)–(volume of water absorbed by the waste).

Generation Rate after Closure

After the construction of the final cover only the water which can infiltrate through the final cover percolates through the waste and generates leachate. The major quantity of precipitation will be converted to surface run-off and the quantity of leachate generation can be estimated as follows:

Leachate volume = (volume of precipitation)–(volume of surface run-off)-(volume lost through evaporation)–(volume of water absorbed by waste and intermediate soil coverts).

For landfills which do not receive run-off from outside areas, a very approximate estimate of leachate generation can be obtained by assuming it to be 25 to 50 per cent of the precipitation from the active landfill area and as 10 to 15 per cent of the precipitation from covered areas. This is a thumb rule and can only be used for preliminary design.

Liner System

Leachate control within a landfill involves the following steps:

(*a*) prevention of migration of leachate from landfill sides and landfill base to the subsoil by a suitable liner system; and

(*b*) drainage of leachate collected at the base of a landfill to the sides of the landfill and removal of the leachate from within the landfill.

Liner system comprises of a combination of leachate drainage and collection layer(s) and barrier layer(s). A component liner system should have low permeability, should be robust and durable and should be resistant to chemical attacks puncture and rupture. A liner system may comprise of a combination of barrier materials such as natural clays, amended soils and flexible geomembranes. Three types of liner systems are usually adopted and these are described here after:

(*a*) Single Liner System: Such a system comprises of a single primary barrier overlaid by a leachate collection system with an appropriate separation/protection layer. A system of this type is used for a low valnerability landfill.

(*b*) Single Composite Liner System: A composite lines comprises of two barriers, made of different materials, placed in intimate contact with each other to provide a beneficial combined effect of both the barriers usually a flexible geomembrane is placed over a day or amonded soil barrier. A leachate collection system is placed over the composite barrier. Single composite liner system one often the minimum specified lines system for non-hazardous wastes such as MSW.

(*c*) **Double Liner System:** In a double liner system a single liner system is placed twice, one beneth the other. The top barrier (called the primary barrier) is overlaid by a leachate collection system. Beneath the primary barrier, another leachate collection system (often called the leak detection layer) is placed followed by a second barrier (the secondary barrier). This type of system offers double safety and is often used beneath industrial waste landfills. It allows the monitoring of any seepage which may escape the primary barrier layer.

The advantages of a composite liner system are immense and often not widely recognised. The way that a composite liner works is selected and is contrasted with individual geomembranes and soil liners. To achieve good composite action the geomembrane must be placed against the clay with good hydraulic contact. To achieve intimate, contact, the surface of a compacted sort liner on which the geomembrane is placed should be smooth-rolled with a steel-drum roller. All oversize stones on the soils should be removed prior to rolling, Also, the geomembrane should be placed and backfilled in a way that minimizes wrinkles.

On a basis of review of linear system adopted in different countries, it is recommended that for all MSW landfills the foillowing single composite liner system be adopted (waste downwards) as the minimum requirement:

(*a*) A leachate drainage layer 30 cm thick made of granular soil having permeability greater than 10^{-2} cm/sec.

(*b*) A protector layer (of silty soil) 20cm to 30cm thick.

(*c*) A geomembrane of thickness 1.5mm or more.

(*d*) A compacted clay barrier or amended soil barrier of 1m thickness having permeability of less than 10^{-7} cm/sec.

The liner system may have to be stringent in free drainage alluvial soil at locations where water-table level is close to the base of the landfill.

Cut-off Walls

When a landfill is undertaken at shallow depths by an impervious layer, vertical cut-off walls may be constructed around a landfill to intercept off-site migration, cut-off walls are physical barriers (typical made of bentonite or bentonite soil mine) and such barriers are aided by active pumping used to remove leachates from within the perimeter of the cut-off wall.

Liners for Steep Slopes and Vertical Quarry Faces

Liners along very steep slopes and vertical faces require site specific solutions which are usually compton.

Leachate Drainage, Collection and Removal

A leachate collection system comprises of a drainage layer, a perforated pipe collector system, sump collection area and a removal system.

The leachate drainage layer is usually 30cm thick, has a slope of 2 per cent or higher and a permeability of greater than 0.01 cm/sec. A system of perforated pipes and sumps are provided within the drainage layer. The pipe spacing is governed by the requirement that the leachate head should not be greater than the drainage layer thickness. Figure 5.2 shows the typical layout of pipes and sumps.

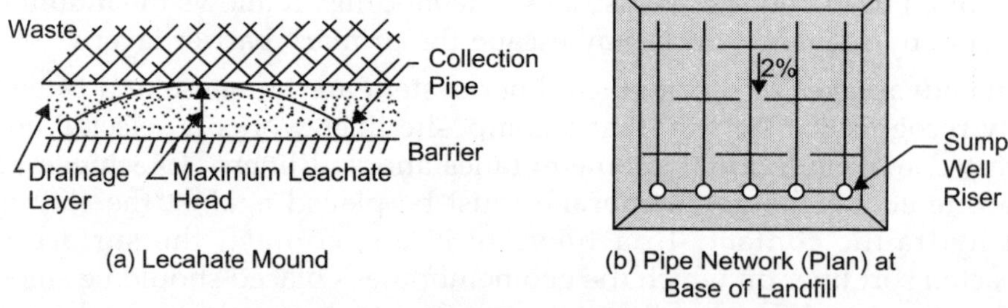

Fig. 5.2 Leachate Collection Pipe Network

Leachate is icmoved from the land felt (Fig. 5.3) by:

(*a*) Pumping in vertical wells or chimneys;

(*b*) Pumping in side slope rises;

(*c*) By gravity drains rough the base of a landfill in above ground and sloped landfills.

Side slope risers are prepared to vertical wells to avoid any down drag problems. Submersible pumps have been used for several years, educator pumps are also being increasingly used. In some landfills, the leachate is stored in a holding tank (for a few days) before being sent for treatment.

The possibility of fall is efficiency of the drainage system due to clogging associated with solid deposits and microbial growth is now well recognized. A number of options including back flushing or break through water after leachate head build up need to be investigated at the design stage.

The design steps for the leachate collection system are:

(*i*) Finalization of layout pipe network and sumps in conjunction with drainage layer slopes of two per cent;

(*ii*) Estimation of pipe diameter and spacing on the basis of estimated leachate quantity and maximum permissible leachate head;

(*iii*) Estimating the size of sumps and pumps;

(*iv*) Design of wells/side slopes risers for leachate removal; and

(*v*) Design of a holding tank.

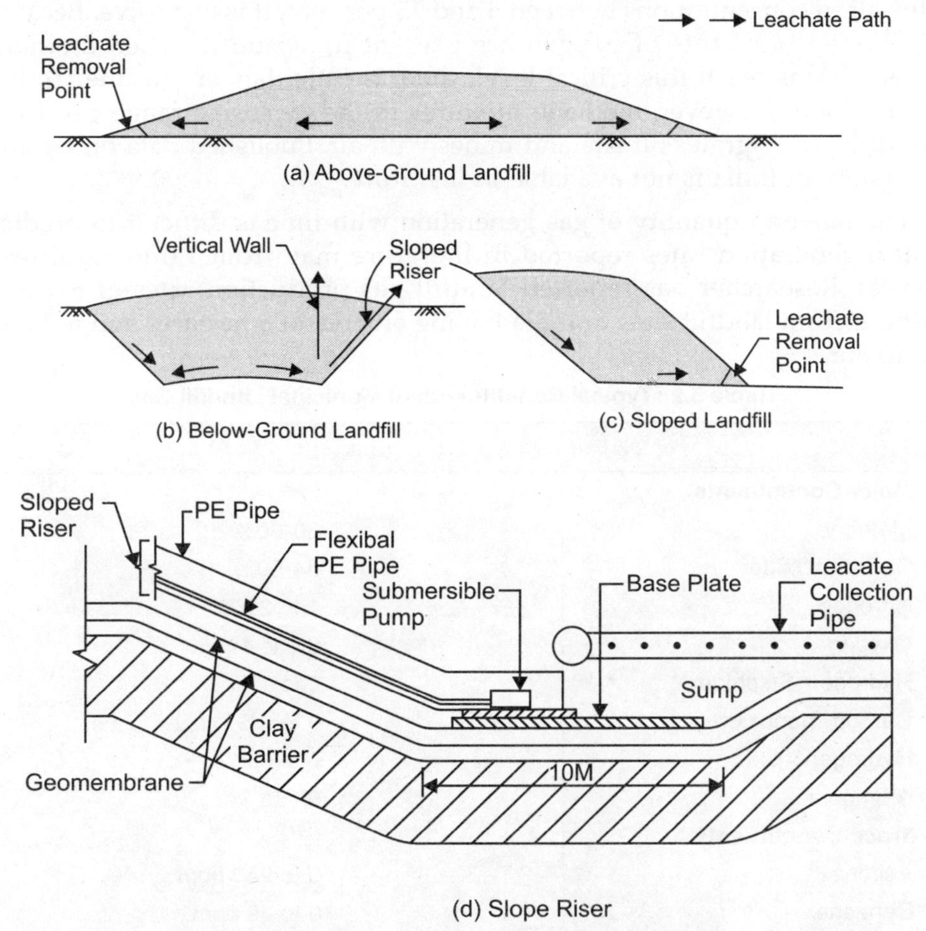

Fig. 5.3 Leachate Drainage and Removal System

Estimation of Landfill Gas Quality and Quantity

Landfill gas is generated as a product of waste biodegradation. Biological degradation of the waste may occur in the presence of oxygen (aerobic bacteria), in an environmental devoid of oxygen (anaerobic bacteria), or with vary little oxygen (facultative anaerobic bacteria).

In all cases organic waste is broken down by enzymes produced by bacteria in a manner comparable to food digestion. Considerable heat is generated by these reactions with methane, carbon dioxide and other gases as the by products. The typical percentage distribution of gases found in a MSW landfill is reported in Table 5.1. Methane and carbon dioxide are the principal gases produced from the anaerobic decomposition of the biogedradable organic waste components in MSW. When methane is present in the air in concentrations between 5 and 15 per cent, it is explosive. Because only limited amounts of oxygen are present in a landfill when methane concentrations reach this critical level, there is little danger that the landfill welt explode. However, methane mixtures in the explosive range can form if landfill gas migrates off site and mines with air. Published data on landfill gas quality in India is not available in literature.

The rate and quantity of gas generation with time is difficult to predict. Typical generation rates reported in literature may from 1.0 to 8.0 litres/kg/year. Researcher has reported landfill gas production rates of 6.0cu.m per hour from landfill sites in India having an area of 8 hectares and a depth of 5 to 8m.

Table 5.2 : Typical Constituents of Municipal Landfill Gas

Constituent	Range (Percentage of Concentration)
Major Constituents	
Methane	30-60%
Carbondioxide	34-60%
Nitrogen	1 to 21%
Oxygen	0.1 to 1%
Hydrogen Sulphide	0 to 1%
Carbon monoxide	0 to 2%
Hydrogen	0 to 0.2%
Ammonia	0.1 to 1%
Trace Constituents	
Acitone	0 to 240 ppm
Benzene	0 to 39 ppm
Vinyl chloride	0.44 ppm
Toluene	8 to 280 ppm
Chloroform	0 to 12 ppm
Dichloromethane	1 to 620 ppm
Dielhylene chloride	0 to 20 ppm
Vinyl Acetate	0 to 240 ppm
Trichloroethane	0 to 13 ppm
Perchloroethane	0 to 19 ppm
Others	Variable

Landfill gas can move upward or downward is a landfill depending on their density. Although most of the methane escapes to the atmosphere, both methane and carbon dioxide have been found at concentrations up to 40 per cent at lateral distances of 100m or more from the edges of unlined landfills. For unvented landfills, the extent of this lateral movement varies with the characteristics of the cover material and the surrounding soil. If methane is vented in an uncontrolled manner, it can accumulate (because its density is less than that of air) below buildings or in other closed space close to a sanitary landfill with proper venting, methane should not pose a problem (except that it is a greenhouse gas). Carbon dioxide, in the other hand is troublesome because of its high density. The concentration of carbon dioxide in the lower portions of a landfill may be high for years.

Gas control within a landfill site involves the following features:

(*a*) a containment system which encloses the gas within the site and prevents migration outside the landfill;

(*b*) a system (passive or active) for collecting and removing landfill gas from with in the landfill and in particular from the perimeter of the landfill;

(*c*) a system for flaring or utilizing the colleted gas with adequate back-up facilities.

Surface Water Drainage System

Surface water management is required to ensure that rain-water run off does not drain into the waste from surrounding areas and that there is no water logging/ponding on covers of landfills.

These objectives should be activated by the following:

(*a*) Rainwater running off slopes above and outside the landfill area should be intercepted and channeled to water courses without entering the operational area of the site. This diversion channel may require a low permeability lining to prevent leakage into the landfill;

(*b*) Rainfalling on active tipping areas should be collected separately and managed as leachate, via the leachate collection drain and leachate collection sumps to the leachate treatment and disposal system;

(*c*) Rainfall on areas with in the landfill site but on final covers of phases which have been completed are not actively being used for waste disposal should be diverted o away in drainage channels from an active tipping areas, and directed through a settling pond to remove suspended silt, prior to discharge;

(*d*) Any drainage channels odourous constructed on the restored landfill surface should be able to accommodate settlement, resist erosion and cope with localized storm conditions;

(*e*) The final cover should be provided a slope of 3 to 5 per cent for proper surface water drainage;

(*f*) All interceptor channels, drainage channels and settling ponds (storm water basins) should be designed by a hydrologist using hydrometerological data.

Site Infrastructure

The following site infrastructure should be provided :

(*a*) Site entrance and fencing;

(*b*) Administrative and site control offices;

(*c*) Access roads;

(*d*) Waste inspection and sampling facility;

(*e*) Equipment workshops and garages;

(*f*) Signs and directions;

(*g*) Water supply;

(*h*) Lighting;

(*i*) Vehicle cleaning facility;

(*j*) Fire fighting equipment.

Site entrance infrastructure should include :

(*a*) A permanent wide entrance road with separate entry and exit lanes and gates;

(*b*) Sufficient length/parking space inside the entrance gate till the weighbridge to prevent queuing of vehicles outside the entrance gate and on to the highway. A minimum road length of 50m inside the entry gate is desirable;

(*c*) A properly landscaped entrance area with a green belt of 20m containing tree plantation for good visual impact;

(*d*) Proper direction signs and lighting at the entrance gate;

(*e*) A perimeter fencing of at least 2m height all around the landfill site with lockable gates to prevent unauthorized access;

(*f*) Full time security guard at the site.

An accurate record of waste inputs is essential. Twin weighbridges to weigh both entry and exit weights may be located on either side of an island on which a weighbridge office room is located. The weighbridge should be located well inside the entrance gate to avoid congestion and queuing at the gate. The weighbridge office should be elevated and the weighbridge operation should be able to see entering vehicles as well as speak to drivers. Raised platforms weighbridges with computerized output and with facility for manual recording of displayed readings are recommended such weighbridges should remain operative during power supply failure.

Administrative and site control offices should include : administrative office building (permanent); site control office (portable) near the active landfill area; stores (permanent) within or near administrative office; welfare facilities, toilets, show room, first-aid room, small temporary accommodation;

infrastructure services, electricity, drinking water supply, telephone, sewerage and drainage system and administrative office and weighbridge office.

The provision of well maintained, high quality site roads is necessary to ensure the free flow of traffic and a fast turn around of vehicles. The construction details of three types of roads are required *i.e.* main access road (permanent); arterial road (permanent) and temporary road.

POLLUTION PREVENTION DURING OPERATION

Measures are needed to ensure that the landfill operation does not adversely effect local environment within and outside the landfill. Operators may appoint community liaison officers to be available to visit complainants and establish the nature and source of the problem. This is reported to the site manager so that corrective measures can be taken.

Traffic

Heavy lorry traffic can give rise to nuisance, damage to road surface and verges and routing problems. The following guidelines are helpful:

(*a*) Routing to avoid residential areas;

(*b*) Using one-way router to avoid traffic conflict in narrow roads;

(*c*) Carrying out road improvements for example strengthening or widening roads, improved provision of footpaths, improvement of sight lines, provision of passing places, and provision of new roads;

(*d*) Limiting the number of vehicle movements;

(*e*) Restrictions on traffic movement hours which are staggered with respect to peak traffic hours.

Noise

Adverse impacts on the local community from noise may arise from a number of sources including—throughput of vehicles and fixed and mobile plant, for example compators, generators at the site. Peripheral noise abatement site measuring should be adopted.

Odour

Offensive odours at landfill sites may emanate from a number of sources, including waste materials, which have decomposed significantly prior to landfilling, leachate and leachate treatment systems and landfill gas.

Good landfill practices will greatly reduce general site smell and reduce impact odours which could lead to complaints from the local community, site users and site staff. Good practices includes:

(*a*) adequate compaction;

(*b*) speedy disposal and burial of malodorous wastes;

(*c*) effective use of appropriate types of daily cover;

(*d*) progressive capping and restoration;

(*e*) effective landfill gas management;

(*f*) effective leachate management; and

(*g*) consideration of prevailing wind direction when planning leachate treatment plants, gas flares and direction of tipping.

Litter

Poor litter control both on and off site is particularly offensive to neighbours. Good operational practice should be adhered to in terms of waste discharge, placement, and compaction for controlling litter include:

(*a*) Consideration of prevailing wind direction and strength when planning the filling direction and sequence;

(*b*) Strategically placed mobile screen close to the tipping area or on the nearest down wind crest;

(*c*) Temporary banks and bunds immediately adjacent to the tipping area;

(*d*) Permanent catch fences and netting to trap wind blown litter;

(*e*) Restricting in coming vehicles to only those which are sheeted and secured well reduce litter problems on the high ways.

Litter pickers should be employed to collect litter which escapes the preventative measures. Litter screens, fences, nets and perimeter ditches should be maintained free of litter.

Bird Control

Birds are attracted to landfill sites in large numbers, particularly where sites receive appreciable amounts of food wastes. Usually only large birds such as eagles gulls are regarded as a nuisance. Bird control techniques should be carefully planned taking into account the species likely to be affected. Measures which can be used to mitigate bird nuisance include the employment of good landfill practice, working in small active areas and progressive prompt covering of waste, together with the use of bird scaring techniques. Measures involving explosions or distress calls have inherently adverse environmental impacts in terms of noise.

Vermin and Other Pests

Landfills have potential to harbour flies and vermin, particularly where the waste contains food materials. Modern land filling techniques including prompt emplacement, consolidation and covering of wastes in well defined cells are effective in the prevention of infestation by rodents and insects. Rats and flies are the main pests which require control. Sites with extensive non-operational land can become injected with rabbits.

Effective measures to deal with rodent infestation include regular visits by post control constructors or fully trained operatives. The use of insecticides on exposed faces and flannels of the tipping are, by spraying and fogging is an effective means of exterminating insects.

Dust

Dust from landfill operations is mainly a problem during periods of dry wheather but can also arise from dustry waste as it is tipped. Dust is generally associated with:

(*a*) site preparation and restoration activities

(*b*) the disposal of waste comprising of five particales for examples powders; and

(*c*) traffic dust.

Dust suspension can be effected by

(*a*) limiting vechicles;

(*b*) spraying roads with water; and

(*c*) spraying site and poor type waste with water.

Mud on the Road

Mud on the public highway is one of the most common causes of public complaint. It is therefore in the interest of the landfill operator to provide adequate wheel cleaning facilities to ensure that mud is not carried off site by vechicles.

Disposal of Construction and Demolition Waste

Being predominantly inert in nature, construction and demolition waste does not create chemical or biochemical pollution. Hence maximum effort should be made to reuse and recycle them. The material can be used for filling/levelling of low-lying areas. In the industrialized countries, special landfills are sometimes created for inert waste, which are normally located in bandoned mines and quarries. The same can be attempted in our country also for sites, which are located near open mining quarries or mines where normally sand is used as the filling material. However, proper sampling of the material for its physical and chemical characteristics has to be done. For evaluating its use under the given circumstances.

Disposal of Industrial Waste

Depending upon the characterstics of the waste, different types of disposal methods can be used for hazardous and non-hazards industrial wastes. The most predominant and widely practiced methods for wastes disposal are:

(*a*) Landfill;

(*b*) Incineration; and

(*c*) Composting.

6

Solid Waste Management

Planning and designing of collection, processing and disposal of solid waste require the knowledge of waste characteristics.

GENERATION

The daily per capita solid waste generated in India ranges from about 100 grams in small towns to 500 grams in large towns. The recyclable content of wastes ranges from 13 per cent to 20 per cent (Central Pollution Control Board 1994/95). Though few reliable statistics on solid waste generation are available at the national level, an attempt has been made to collect and collate data from different sources to get some idea of the trends in generation and management of solid wastes.

A primary survey in 1971 estimated that the urban populace generated 374 grams of solid waste per head per day. Another survey in 1981 put the figure at 432 grams and yet another in 1995 at 456 grams. Based on these estimates and taking the annual growth rate in per capita generation as one per cent for pre-1980 and 1.33 per cent for post-1990, the urban MSW generated for the years 1947 to 1997 are shown in Table 6.1.

Table 6.1 : Waste generated (MT) annually in Indian cities: 1947 to 1997

Year	1947	1951	1961	1971	1981	1991	1997
Urban population (millions)	56.9	62.44	78.94	109.1	159.5	217.2	274
Daily per capita generation (grams)	295	305	340	375	430	460	490
Total waste generated	**6**	**.7**	**10**	**15**	**25**	**37**	**48**

The waste thus computed included all types of waste that ends up in community bins placed in residential, commercial, and industrial areas. However, tins does not include the waste that is recycled. Therefore, as a conservative estimate, the total MSW generated in urban India in 1997 can be put at about 48 million tonnes.

COLLECTION

Waste is usually collected in small bins by those who generate the waste. Waste from these bins is then transferred to community bins either by those who generate it or by private or municipal workers. Waste from community bins is collected by trucks and carried to the disposal site. It takes anywhere from 3 to 7 days for the waste to be disposed off from the time it is generated. The collection, transportation and disposal off waste are labour-intensive activities because modern, automated systems are not used. In recent years, the number of cities that are short of municipal workers has increased The prime reason for this is the government's policy to restrict employment. As a result, on an average, less than three-fourths of the waste is collected.

TRANSPORTATION

Solid waste is usually transported in open trucks, compaction vehicles, tractor-trailers, or carrier-containers. However, open trucks are used by most of the municipal corporations; in small towns, even bullock carts are employed for this purpose. The vehicles are normally owned and maintained by municipal authorities. Lately, however, a few corporations have resorted to hiring vehicles from private contractors. Hired vehicles have been found to work more effectively and efficiently if monitored and held accountable for the services rendered by them. The concept is catching on because it is cost-effective.

On an average, a cubic metre of MSW at the generation site weighs about 500 kg (Bhide and Sundaresan 1983). Considering the daily per capita generation rate of 480 grams, the volume of waste required to be transported is about 960 cubic metres per million population. Assuming that a truck makes three trips in a day, the minimum transport capacity required is about 320 cubic metres per million population every day. It is clear that about 70 per cent of Indian cities do not have such capacity. The figure might be even higher, considering that the fleet in most cities is old and its performance very poor. The uncollected waste normally finds its way into sewers; some of it is eaten by cattle; and some lies about for a few days before sweepers collect it together and bum it in the open.

DISPOSAL OF WASTE

As cities are growing in size with a rise in the population, the amount of waste generated is increasing becoming unmanageable. The wastes are normally brought to a designated landfill site, normally a low-lying area on the outskirts of a city. The choice of a site is more a matter of what is available than what is suitable. Only a few cities follow such good practices as organized tipping of wastes, using mechanized equipment for levelling and compacting the wastes, and covering the top layer with earth before compacting it further. Of late, some cities have taken to composting the wastes. The lifespan of the existing disposal sites varies from 1 to 30 years.

Industrial wastes have generally been a neglected area of management. Of late, slag from steel industry and fly ash from thermal power plants are being utilized by the cement industry. However, only 1-2 per cent of fly ash and 30 per cent-60 per cent of blast furnace slag are utilized.

Industrial solid waste poses a serious threat to the environment because the disposal is largely uncontrolled; dumping the industrial waste on public land or making it a part of MSW is quite common. Proper methods of waste disposal have to be undertaken to ensure that it does not affect the environment around the area or cause health hazards to the people living there.

At the household-level proper segregation of waste has to be done and it should be ensured that all organic matter is kept aside for composting, which is undoubtedly the best method for the correct disposal of this segment of the waste. In fact, the organic part of the waste that is generated decomposes more easily, attracts insects and causes disease. Organic waste can be composted and then used as a fertilizer. The methods of treatment and disposal of hazardous waste as practised in India are given in Table 6.2. Chemical processes to destroy hazardous constituents and biotechnological processes to detoxify hazardous components are seldom employed.

Table 6.2 Methods of Waste Disposal in Select Industries Industry

Wastes	Disposal of wastes
Petrochemicals	All sludge and solid wastes from a plant are collected and sent to a disposal site outside the plant.
Paints, varnish, lacquers	Solid waste is collected at point of generation in barrels and given to a contractor for disposal. Date-expired paints are sold off. Waste treatment sludge is disposed of along with other solid wastes.
Dye intermediates	Anually collected and dumped in low-lying areas (naphthalene-based) H acid, G acid, peracids
Ethanolamine	Put in drums and stored underground or incinerated
Ortho-chlorine	Burnt in open pits

The various processes involved in disposal are:

- Source reduction and reuse
- Composting
- Recycling
- Incineration
- Sanitary Landfills

Source Reduction and Reuse

Overview

During the past 50 years, the amount of waste each person creates has almost doubled from 2.7 to 4.4 pounds per day. The most effective way to stop this trend is by preventing waste in the first place.

- **Source Reduction** refers to any change in die design, manufacture, purchase, or use of materials or products (including packaging) to reduce their amount or toxicity before they become municipal solid waste.
- Source reduction also refers to the reuse of products or materials. Waste prevention, also know as 'source reduction,' is the practice of designing, manufacturing, purchasing, or using materials (such as products and packaging) in ways that reduce the amount or toxtcity of trash created. Reusing items is another way to stop waste at the source because it delays or avoids that item's entry in the waste collection and disposal system.

Source reduction, including reuse, can help reduce waste disposal and handling costs, because it avoids the costs of recycling, municipal composting, landfilling, and combustion. Source reduction also conserves resources and reduces pollution, including greenhouse gases that contribute to global warming.

Source Reduction and Reuse Facts

- More than 55 million tons of MSW were source reduced in the United States in 2000.
- Containers and packaging represented approximately 28 per cent of the materials source reduced in 2000, in addition to nondurable goods (*e.g.*, newspapers, clothing) at 17 per cent, durable goods (*e.g.*, appliances, furniture, tyres) at 10 per cent, and other MSW (*e.g.*, yard trimmings, food scraps) at 45 per cent.
- There are more than 6000 reuse centres around the country, ranging from specialized programmes for building materials or unneeded

materials in schools to local programmes such as Goodwill and the Salvation Army, according lo the Reuse Development Organization.

- Between 2 and 5 per cent of the waste stream is potentially reusable according to local studies in Berkeley, California, and Leveiett, Massachusetts.
- Since 1977, the weight of 2-litre plastic soft drink bottles has been reduced from 68 grams each to 51 grams. That means that 250 million pounds of plastic per year has been kept out of the waste stream.
- MSW Facts and Figures provides additional charts and statistics on source reduction, both nationally and by state.

Source Reduction and Reuse Benefits

- **Saves natural resources.** Waste is not just created when consumers throw items away. Throughout the life cycle of a product—from extraction of raw materials to transportation to processing and manufacturing facilities to manufacture and use—waste is generated. Reusing items or making them with less material decreases waste dramatically. Ultimately, less materials will need to be recycled or sent to landfills or waste combustion facilities.
- **Reduces toxicity of waste.** Selecting non-hazardous or less hazardous items is another important component of source reduction. Using less hazardous alternatives for certain items (*e.g.*, cleaning products and pesticides), sharing products that contain hazardous chemicals instead of throwing out left-overs, reading label directions carefully, and using the smallest amount necessary are ways to reduce waste toxicity.
- **Reduces costs.** The benefits of preventing waste go beyond reducing reliance on other forms of waste disposal. Preventing waste also can mean economic savings for communities, businesses, schools, and individual consumers.
- **Communities.** More than 4000 communities have instituted "pay-as-you-throw" programmes where citizens pay for each can or bag of trash they set out for disposal rather than through fee tax base or a flat fee. When these households reduce waste at the source, they dispose of less trash and pay lower trash bills.
- **Businesses.** Industry also has an economic incentive to practice source reduction. When businesses manufacture their products with less packaging, they are buying less raw material. A decrease in manufacturing costs can mean a larger profit margin, with savings that can be passed on to the consumer.

- **Consumers.** Consumers also can share in the economic benefits of source reduction. Buying products in bulk, with less packaging, or that are reusable (not single-use) frequently means a cost savings. What is good for the environment can be good for the pocketbook as well.

Buying Recycled Products

Overview

Creating a strong market for recycled products is key to completing the recycling process or 'closing the loop.' Consumers close the loop when they purchase products made from recycled materials. Governments can promote buying recycled products through their own purchasing programmes and guidelines. Manufacturers can participate as well by using recycled materials in their products.

Identifying Recycled-Content Products

Product labels can be confusing to consumers interested in buying recycled because of the different recycling terminology used. For the use of environmental marketing claims.

- **Recycled-content products** are made from materials that would otherwise have been discarded. Items in this category are made totally or partially from material destined for disposal or recovered from industrial activities—like aluminum soda cans or newspaper. Recycled-content products also can be items that are rebuilt or remanufactured from used products such as toner cartridges or computers.
- **Post-consumer content** refers to material from products that were used by consumers or businesses and would otherwise be discarded as waste. If a product is labeled 'recycled content,' the rest of the product material might have come from excess or damaged items generated during normal manufacturing processes—not collected through a local recycling programme.
- Recyclable products can be collected and remanufactured into new products after they've been used. These products do not necessarily contain recycled materials and only benefit the environment if people recycle them after use. Check with your local recycling programme to determine which items are recyclable in your community.

Recycled Products Shopping List

There are more than 4500 recycled-contenl products available, and this number continues to grow. In fact, many of the products people regularly purchase contain recycled-content. The following list presents just a sampling: Aluminum cans, Newspapers, Cereal boxes, Paper towels, Egg cartons, Carpeting, Motor oil, Car bumpers, Nails, Anything made from steel, Trash bags, Glass containers, Comic books, Laundry detergent boldes. The following product directories and databases provide a more comprehensive list of products and manufacturers.

Buying Recycled Products

There's more to recycling than setting out your recyclables at the curb. In order to make recycling economically feasible, we must buy recycled products and packaging. When we buy recycled products, we create an economic incentive for recyclable materials to be collected, manufactured, and marketed as new products. Buying recycled has both economic and environmental benefits. Purchasing products made from or packaged in recycled materials saves resources for future generations.

Conclusion

In summary, there are four main ways that most city governments in developing countries can enhance waste reduction:

- **Inform citizens about source separation and recycling, and the needs of waste workers:** Extensive public education is needed to develop understanding of the need for further source separation to improve the potential for composting and to remove the stigma of association with waste materials.
- **Promote recycling industries and enterprises.**
- **Divert organics.** The greatest relief for the wasle authority will come from reduction of organics, which implies, in the main, successful composting. Keeping organics pure for composting will require more thorough source separation than is done at present.
- **Advocate key areas for waste reduction at the manufacturing level** (*e.g.*, reduction of plastic packaging; coding of plastics to improve recycling).

Waste generation and waste reduction reflect many complex economic and social factors. No city or town can adopt recommendations in a vacuum, each must examine its own wastes, and the potential for extending waste reduction. There are many possible ways to implement the general dictum that waste reduction should be the first principle of solid waste management. Humane concern for waste workers must temper the drive to greater efficiency. During periods of technical change, there are winners and losers, and in the field of materials recovery there should be attention to those who 'lose out' as operations become more efficient. In most cases, the resulting municipal strategy will be a mix of private and public sector activities. Highly toxic wastes are sometimes destroyed by controlled incineration but more commonly, small quantities of sludge are burnt along with factory garbage in open pits. Secured landfilling of containers of wastes, again, is nol as common as uncontrolled dumping, which is the most common practice. Industrial waste is disposed along with municipal solid waste in industrial agglomerations.

What you can do to reduce solid waste

- Carry your own cloth or jute bag when you go shopping.
- Say no to all plastic bags as far as possible.
- Reduce the use of paper bags also.
- Reuse the soft drinks polybottles for storing water.
- Segregate the waste in the house—keep two garbage bins and see to it that the biodegradable and the non-biodegradable is put into separate bins and dispose off separately.
- Dig a compost pit in your garden and put all the biodegradables into it.
- See to it that all garbage is thrown into the municipal bin as the collection is generally done from there.
- When you go out do not throw paper and other wrappings or even leftover food here and there, make sure that it is put in the correct place, that is into a dustbin.
- As far as possible try to sell all the recyclable items that are not required to the *kabariwala* (person who trades in waste).

Composting

Another form of recycling is composting. Composting is the controlled biological decomposition of organic matter, such as food and yard wastes, into humus, a soil-like material. Composting is nature's way of recycling organic waste into new soil, which can be used in vegetable and (lower gardens, landscaping, and many ther applications.

Contents of Composting

Overview

Composting is the controlled decomposition of organic materials, such as leaves, grass, and food scraps, by microorganisms. The result of this decomposition process is compost, a crumbly, earthy-smelling, soil-like material. Yard trimmings and food scraps make up about 25 per cent of the waste US. households generate, so composting can greatly reduce the amount of waste that ends up in landfills or incinerators.

Process Preparation: What to Put in the Mix

These are some items that can be put in a composting bin. Some food products should not be included because they can attract pests or compromise the quality of the compost. This list is not meant to be all inclusive.

Materials to Include

Fruit and vegetable scraps, Egg shells, Coffee grounds with filters, Tea bags, Fireplace ash, Leaves, Grass, Yard clippings, Vacuum cleaner lint wool and cotton rags, Sawdust, non-recyclable paper.

Materials to Exclude Meats

Dairy foods, Fats, Oils (including peanut butter and mayonnaise) Grease Pet excrement, Fish scraps, Diseased plants, Bones.

Composting Process

Compost contains both carbon and nitrogen sources, which can be simplified as browns for carbon (*e.g.*, leaves, straw, woody materials) and greens for nitrogen (*e.g.*, grass and food scraps). Adequate sources of carbon and nitrogen are important for microorganism growth and energy. The ideal ratio is 30 parts brown to 1 part green. Odour and other problems can occur if the ratio or any of the factors discussed below are not in the correct balance. The decomposition of organic materials in composting involves both physical and chemical processes. During decomposition, organic materials are broken down through the activities and appetites of various invertebrates that will naturally appear in compost, such as mites, millipedes, beetles, sowbugs, earwigs, earthworms, slugs, and snails. These microorganisms need adequate moisture and oxygen to degrade the organic materials in the most efficient manner. Microbes in the pile create considerable heat and essentially 'cook' the compost. Temperatures between 90 and 140°F are common in properly maintained compost piles, but may not reach these levels in backyard compost piles. These high temperatures are necessary for rapid composting as well as for destroying weed seeds, insect larvae, and potentially harmful bacteria. When the compost is finished, it has a crumbly texture throughout the pile.

Composting Facts and Figures

Red wigglers (*i.e.*, ihe worms used in vermicomposling) eat iheir weight in organic matter each day. More than 67 per cent of the municipal solid waste produced in the United States (including paper) is compostable material. There are more than 3,800 yard trimmings composting facilities nationwide.

MSW Facts and Figures provides additional information such as the number of states with yard waste bans.

Opportunities

Whether composting occurs in the backyard, at a community site with yard trimmings, or in an industrial facility with mixed MSW, the resulting compost is a valuable product. Not only can compost be used as a soil additive for backyard gardens and farm lands or to beautify highways and other landscaping projects, but it also has many innovative uses.

Types of Composting

The various types of Composting are describes as below:

Backyard Composting

Hundreds of thousands of individuals across the country compost in their own backyards, typically in a fenced off area or bin. Backyard composting provides a convenient way to reduce the volume of trash a household produces. It also provides a valuable product that can enhance the soil and increase the growth and health of the yard.

Yard Trimmings Composting

Composting also occurs on a large scale, operated by private sector firms or community public works departments. At these sites, the compostable material is taken to a central location. There, it is typically processed in aerated windrows, where organics are formed into rows or long piles. Some sites will add compostable MSW into the mix to keep items out of the landfill. The finished compost can be sold, given away, or used by the company or municipality in local landscaping projects.

Mixed MSW Composting

Composting of mixed municipal solid waste is another option. This generally occurs at a medium-to-large scale facility, operated by private sector firms or community public works departments. Generally, mixed MSW is received at the site. Recyclables such as glass and aluminum, and non-compostables are removed early in the process. The remaining organic material is composted, generally using aerated windrows. In-vessel composting, where the material is left lo decompose while enclosed in a temperature and moisture controlled chamber, is another possibility. Final screening steps remove any remaining plastic film and similar contents. The finished compost can be sold, given away, or used by the company or municipality in local landscaping projects.

Vermicomposting

Although not significant in terms of waste diversion, vermicomposting is being used in some places and is popular in classrooms as a teaching tool. This method of composting uses a container of food scraps and a special kind of earthworm known as a red wiggler. Over time, the food is replaced with worm droppings, a rich brown matter that serves as an excellent natural plant food. Vermicomposting requires less space than normal composting methods, and is, therefore, ideal for classrooms, apartments, and other settings in high-density urban areas.

Bio-solids Composting

EPA endorses the composting of biosolids (or sewage sludge) as a way of managing this material. EPA characterizes bios-olids composting and offers guidance and technical assistance via the Office of Wastewater Management in EPA's Office of Water.

Major Factors to be Considered in Composting

- **Siting:** Compost facilities must be reasonably close to the input stream and the potential users, but must be sited in a way that is compatible with the desires of the nearby community.
- **Input stream:** Source-separated organics are best, but this is not possible in most developing countries. Mixed waste can be processed to yield acceptable compost.
- **Selection of appropriate technology:** The technology chosen must be adequate for the input stream and for the level of economic development of the country.
- **Scale:** A smaller-scale facility often facilitates careful composting and the formation of a good product.
- **Market development:** Governments generally need to stimulate the compost market. Quality standards are an important element of this.
- **Existing compost practices using compost from dumps and garbage dump farming:** These traditional activities, while often dangerous, could in some instances be safe if an adequate testing programme were in place.

Benefits of Composting

- Keeps organic wastes out of landfills.
- Provides nutrients to the soil.
- Increases beneficial soil organisms (*e.g.*, worms and centipedes).
- Suppresses certainplant diseases.
- Reduce the need for fertilizers and pesticides.
- Protects soil from erosion.
- Assists pollution remediations.
- Compost allows the soil to retain more plant nutrients over a longer period.
- It supplies part of the 16 essential elements needed by the plants.
- It helps reduce the adverse effects of excessive alkalinity, acidity, or the excessive use of chemical fertilizer.

- It makes soil easier to cultivate.
  It helps keep the soil cool in summer and warm in winter.
  It aids in preventing soil erosion by kepping the soil covered.
  It helps in controlling the growth of weeds in the garden.

Recycling

Overview

Recycling is a series of activities that includes collecting recyclable materials mat would otherwise be considered waste, sorting and processing recyclables into raw materials such as fibers, and manufacturing raw materials into new products.

Recycling Process

Collecting and processing secondary materials, manufacturing recycled-content products, and then purchasing recycled products creates a circle or loop that ensures the overall success and value of recycling:

- **Step 1.** ***Collection and Processing:*** Collecting recyclables varies from community to community, but there are four primary methods: curbsidc, drop-off centres, buy-back centres, and deposit/refund programmes. Regardless of the method used to collect the recyclables, the next leg of their journey is usually the same. Recyclables are sent to a materials recovery facility to be sorted and prepared into marketable commodities for manufacturing. Recyclables are bought and sold just like any other commodity, and prices for the materials change and fluctuate with the market.
- **Step 2.** ***Manufacturing:*** Once cleaned and separated, the recyclables are ready to undergo the second part of the recycling loop. More and more of today's products are being manufactured with total or partial recycled content Common household items that contain recycled materials include newspapers and paper towels; aluminum, plastic, and glass soft drink containers; steel cans; and plastic laundry detergent bottles. Recycled materials also are used in innovative applications such as recovered glass in roadway asphalt (glassphalt) or recovered plastic in carpeting, park benches, and pedestrian bridges.
- **Step 3.** ***Parchasing Recycled Products:*** Purchasing recycled products completes the recycling loop. By 'buying recycled,' governments, as well as businesses and individual consumers, each play an important role in making the recycling process a success. As consumers demand more environmentally sound products, manufacturers will continue to meet that demand by producing high-quality recycled products.

- ***Recycling Facts and Figures:*** In 1999, recycling and composting activities prevented about 64 million tons of material from ending up in landfills and incinerators. Today, this country recycles 28 per cent of its waste, a rate that has almost doubled during the past 15 years. While recycling has grown in general, recycling of specific materials has grown even more drastically: 42 per cent of all paper, 40 per cent of all plastic soft drink bottles, 55 per cent of all aluminum beer and soft drink cans, 57 per cent of all steel packaging, and 52 per cent of all major appliances are now recycled. Fifty years ago, only one curbiside recycling programme existed in the United States, which collected several materials at the curb. By 1998, 9,000 curbiside programmes and 12,000 recyclable drop-off centres had sprouted up across the nation. 480 materials recovery facilities had been established to process the collected materials in 1998.
- ***Opportunities:*** For recycling to work, everyone has to participate in each phase of the loop. From government and industry, to organizations, small businesses, and people at home, every American can make recycling a part of their dailyroutine.

Below are some ways in which businesses, local governments, and citizens can get involved:

- Get involved with your local or state recycling organization.
- Buy recycled-content products.
- Local Governments: Improve the efficiency of your collection programme. An EPA resource entitled *Getting More for Less: Improving Collection Efficiency* explains several important strategies for improving efficiency as well as case studies of communities that have reaped the benefits of improved solid waste collection.
- Practice full cost accounting (FCA) to assist with identifying and assessing the costs of solid waste management.
- Identify opportunities to increase recycling rates.
- Citizens *Recycle at home.* Find out if there is a recycling programme in your community. If so, participate in the program by separating and pulling out your recyclables for curbiside pickup or taking them to your local drop-off or buy-back centre.
- *Shop smarter.* Use products in containers that can be recycled in your community and items that can be repaired or reused. Also, support recycling markets by buying and using products made from recycled materials.
- Typical materials that are recycled include batteries, recycled at a rate of 94 per cent, paper and paperboard at 45 per cent, and yard

trimmings at 57 per cent. These materials and others may be recycled through curbiside programmes, drop-off centres, buy-back programmes, and deposit systems.

- Recycling prevents the emission of many greenhouse gases and water pollutants, saves energy, supplies valuable raw materials to industry, creates jobs, stimulates the development of greener technologies, conserves resources for our children's future, and reduces the need for new landfills and combustors.
- Recycling also helps reduce greenhouse gas emissions that affect global climate. In 1996, recycling of solid waste in the United States prevented the release of 33 million tons of carbon into the air-roughly the amount emitted annually by 25 million cars.

Benefits of Recycling

Recycling not only makes sense from an environmental standpoint, but also makes good financial sense. For example, creating aluminum cans from recycled aluminum is far less energy-intensive, and less costly, than mining the raw materials and manufacturing new cans from scratch.

Because recycling is clearly good for human health, the nation's economy, and the environment, many people wonder why the federal government does not simply mandate recycling. The primary reason is that recycling is a local issue—the success and viability of recycling depends on a community's resources and structure. A community must consider the costs of a recycling programme, as well as the availability of markets for its recovered materials. In some areas, not enough resources exist to make recycling an economically feasible option. State governments can assess local conditions and set appropriate recycling mandates:

- Conserves resources for our children's future.
- Prevents emissions of many greenhouse gases and water pollutants.
- Saves energy.
- Supplies valuable raw materials to industry.
- Creates jobs.
- Stimulates the development of greener technologies.
- Reduces the need for new landfills and incinerators.
- Recycling turns materials that would otherwise become waste into valuable resources. In addition, it generates a host of environmental, financial, and social benefits.
- Materials like glass, metal, plastics, and paper are collected, separated and sent to facilities that can process them into new materials or products.

Recycling is one of the best environmental success stories of the late 20th century. Recycling, including composting, diverted 68 million tons of material away from landfills and incinerators in 2001, up from 34 million tons in 1990. By 1999, more than 9000 curbside collection programmes served roughly half of the American population. Curbiside programmes, along with drop-off and buy-back centres, resulted in a diversion of about 30 per cent of the nation's solid waste in 2001.

Ways to Reuse

1. Think about ways of reusing things before you recycle or dump them

- **Plastics and glass:** You can wash and reuse plastic and glass containers for storage and there are many things you can do to reduce your mountain of plastic bags—check out our recycling tips for ideas.
- **Textiles (rags and old clothes):** Take clothes you don't want to your local opportunity shop or put them in a clothing bin. Rags are still useful so pop them in the clothing bin as well.
- **Furniture:** Aucklanders threw out 990,000 tonnes of rubbish in 1999. That's 842 kilograms per person and around 65 per cent of it could've been recycled or composted instead. Take old furniture to a second hand store, donate it to the local opportunity shop or take it to the recycling centre at your local landfill or transfer station.
- **Paint:** Donate unwanted paint to community groups, schools. If you can't find someone to use it up, let the paint dry out and recycle the container out or dispose of it with your rubbish.

2. Check whether it can actually be recycled in your area: Cardboard, paper, glass, cans and type 1 and 2 plastics can be recycled in most areas.

- **Glass:** You may be able to put out glass if you have kerbiside recycling and some landfills and transfer stations have bins for recycling glass. Remember, you can only recycle food containers (bottles and jars)—you can't recycle light bulbs, drinking glasses, mugs, cookware or window glass.

- **Paper and cardboard:** You should be able to put out paper and cardboard if you have kerbiside recycling and most landfills and transfer stations have bins for recycling paper and cardboard. Remember, you can't recycle paper or cardboard contaminated with food or other stuff (like pizza boxes).

- **Food and drink cans:** You may be able to put out aluminium and steel cans if you have kerbiside recycling and most landfills and transfer stations have bins for recycling cans.

- **Plastic:** You may be able to put out plastics if you have kerbiside recycling and most landfills and transfer stations have bins for recycling plastic. Most areas recycle plastics type 1 and 2 and some areas take other types as well.

- **Chemicals and used oil:** Contact your local council to find out what services are available in your area for disposing of unwanted chemicals or used oil.

3. Make sure right materials go in the right recycling bin: Look on the recycling bin to see what should go in it. There may be separate bins for different coloured glass or for different plastic types.

Sanitary Landfills

Landfills are generally located in urban areas where a large amount of waste is generated and has to be dumped in a common place. Unlike an open dump, it is a pit that is dug in the ground. The garbage is dumped and the pit is covered thus preventing the breeding of flies and rats. At the end of each clay, a layer of soil is scattered on top of it and some mechanism, usually an earth-moving equipment is used to compress the garbage, which now forms a cell. Thus, every day, garbage is dumped and becomes a cell. After the landfill is full, the area is covered with a thick layer of mud and the site can thereafter be developed as a parking lot or a park.

Landfills have many problems. All types of waste is dumped in landfills and when water seeps through them it gets contaminated and in turn pollutes the surrounding area. This contamination of groundwater and soil through landfills is known as leaching.

An alternative to landfills which will solve the problem of leaching to some extent is a **sanitary landfill** which is more hygienic and built in a methodogical manner. These are lined with materials that are impermeable such as plastics and clay, and are also built over impermeable soil. Constructing sanitary landfills is very costly and they are have their own problems. Some authorities claim that often the plastic liner develops cracks as it reacts with various chemical solvents present in the waste.

The rate of decomposition in sanitary landfills is also extremely variable. This can be due to the for that less oxygen is available as the garbage is compressed very tightly. It has also been observed that some biodegradable materials do not decompose in a landfill. Another major problem is the development of methane gas, which occurs when little oxygen is present, *i.e.* during anaerobic decomposition. In some countries, the methane being produced from sanitary landfills is tapped and sold as fuel.

Incineration

Incineration Plants

This process of burning waste in large furnaces is known as incineration. In these plants the recyclable material is segregated and the rest of the material is burnt. At the end of the process all that is left behind is ash. During the process some of the ash floats out with the hot air. This is called fly ash. Both the fly ash and the ash that is left in the furnace after burning have high concentrations of dangerous toxins such as dioxins and heavy metals. Disposing of this ash is a problem. The ash that is buried at the landfills leaches the area and cause severe contamination.

Burning garbage is not a clean process as it produces tonnes of toxic ash and pollutes the air and water. A large amount of the waste that is burnt here can be recovered and recycled. In feet, at present, incineration is kept as the last resort and is used mainly for treating the infectious waste.

Questionnaire on Disposal of SW

- Is recycling worthwhile?

  Recycling is one of the best environmental success stories of the late 20th century. Recycling, which includes composting, diverted nearly 70 million tons of material away from landfills and incinerators in 2000, up from 34 million tons in 1990-doubling in just 10 years. Recycling turns materials that would otherwise become waste into valuable resources. As a matter of fact, collecting recyclable materials is just the first step in a series of actions that generate a host of financial, environmental, and societal returns. There are several key benefits to recycling:

Benefits of Recycling

- Protects and expands U.S. manufacturing jobs and increases U.S. competitiveness in the global marketplace.
- Reduces the need for landfilling and incineration.
- Saves energy and prevents pollution caused by the extraction and processing of virgin materials and the manufacture of products using virgin materials.
- Decreases emissions of greenhouse gases that contribute to global climate change.
- Conserves natural resources such as timber, water, and minerals.
- Helps sustain the environment for future generations.

• What costs community male—for recycling or throwing trash away?

The answer to this question will vary depending on where you live, and comparing recycling programme and waste disposal costs is a complex-undertaking. Disposal fees for landfills, waste transfer stations, and incinerators vary across the country, but in many areas, particularly on the heavily populated East Coast, they are significant expenses. Costs and returns for recycling programmes also vary greatly, depending on the local resources and demand for the recovered materials. Recycling does cost money, but so does waste disposal. Communities must pay to collect trash and manage a landfill or incinerator and so also should expect to pay for recycling. Assessing how recycling will impact your community requires a full appraisal off the environmental and economic benefits and costs of recycling, as compared to the one-way consumption of resources from disposing of used products and packaging in landfills and incinerators. Analyzing all of these factors together will help you determine if recycling is more cost effective in your community.

• If there is plenty of landfill space, then why should I recycle?

Recycling offers a host of environmental, economic, and societal benefits. While landfill space is plentiful on the national level, some areas of the United States, particularly the heavily populated East Coast, have less landfill capacity and higher landfill costs.

Communities can make money and avoid high disposal costs by selling certain recyclable materials. Markets for recovered materials fluctuate, however—as markets do for all commodities—depending on a variety of economic conditions. Recycling makes good economic sense. Simply put, recycling creates jobs and generates valuable revenue for the United States. According to the U.S. Recycling Economic Information Study, more than 56,000 recycling and reuse establishments in the United States employ approximately 1.1 million people, generate an annual payroll of $37 billion, and gross $236 billion in annual revenues. According to the report, the number of workers in the recycling industry is comparable to the automobile and truck manufacturing industry and is significantly larger than mining and waste management and disposal industries. In addition, wages for workers in the recycling industry are notably higher than the national average for all industries, according to the report.

• How does recycling save energy?

Harvesting, extracting, and processing the raw materials used to manufacture new products is an energy-intensive activity. Reducing or nearly eliminating the need for these processes, therefore, achieves huge savings in energy. Recycling aluminum cans, for example, saves 95 per cent of the energy required to make the same amount of aluminum from its virgin source, bauxite. The amount of energy saved differs by material, but almost all recycling processes achieve significant energy savings compared to production using virgin materials.

In 2000, recycling resulted in an annual energy savings of at least 660 trillion BTUs, which equals the amount of energy used in 6 million households annually. In 2005, recycling is conservatively projected to save 900 trillion BTUs, equal to the annual energy use of 9 million households.

• What effects do waste prevention and recycling have on global warming?

Everyone knows that reducing waste is good for the environment because it conserves natural resources. What many people don't know is that solid waste reduction and recycling also have an impact on global climate change.

The manufacture, distribution, and use of producls—as well as management of the resulting waste—all result in greenhouse gas emissions. Greenhouse gases, which trap heat in the upper atmosphere, occur naturally and help create climates ihai sustain life on our planet. Increased concentrations of these gases can contribute to rising global temperatures, sea level changes, and other climate changes.

Waste prevention and recycling—jointly referred to as waste reduction-help us belter manage—the solid waste we generate. But reducing waste is a potent strategy for reducing greenhouse gases because it can:

- ***Reduce emissions from energy consumption.*** Recycling saves energy. Manufacturing goods from recycled materials typically requires less energy than producing goods from virgin materials. When people reuse goods or when products are made with less material, less energy is needed to extract, transport and process raw materials and to manufacture products. When energy demand decreases, fewer fossil fuels are burned and less carbon dioxide is emitted into the atmosphere.
- ***Reduce emissions from incinerators.*** Recycling and waste prevention divert materials from incinerators and thus reduce greenhouse gas emissions from waste combustion.
- ***Reduce methane emissions from landfills.*** Waste prevention and recycling (including composting) divert organic wastes from landfills, reducing the methane that would be released if these materials decomposed in a landfill. Increase storage of carbon in forests. Trees absorb carbon dioxide from the atmosphere and store it in-wood in a process called "carbon sequestration." Waste prevention and recycling paper products allows more trees to remain standing in the forest, where they can continue to remove carbon dioxide from the atmosphere.

• What product is taking up the most space in US landfills?

The item most frequently encountered in MSW landfills is plain old paper-on average, it accounts for more than 40 per cent of a landfill's contents. This proportion has held steady for decades and in some landfills has actually risen. Newspapers alone can take up as much as 13 per cent of the space in US landfills.

Organic materials, including paper, do not easily biodegrade once they are disposed of in a landfill. Paper is many times more resistant to deterioration when compacted in a landfill than when it is in open contact with the atmosphere. Researcher who runs the Garbage Project, has shown that, when excavated from a landfill, newspapers from the 1960s can be intact and readable.

• What materials are not safe to throw in my trash?

Chances are, there are certain items or products in your house that you should not throw out in the trash. Many common household items, such as paint, cleaners, oils, batteries, and pesticides, contain hazardous components. Leftover portions of these products are called household hazardous waste (HHW). These products, if mishandled, can be dangerous to human health and the environment. Certain types of HHW can cause physical injury to sanitation workers, contaminate septic tanks or wastewater treatment systems if poured down drains or toilets, and present hazards to children and pets if left around the house. Some communities have special programmes that allow residents to dispose of HHW separately. Others allow disposal of properly prepared HHW in trash, particularly those areas that do not yet have special HHW collection programmes in place. Call your local Department of Sanitation or Department of Public Works for instructions on proper disposal. Follow their instructions and also read product labels for disposal directions to reduce the risk of products exploding, igniting, leaking, mixing with other chemicals, or posing other hazards on the way to a disposal facility. Even empty containers that used to contain HHW can pose hazards because of the residual chemicals inside.

• How do I know what materials are recyclable in my community, and where can I take these materials to be recycled?

Most communities employ recycling coordinators—government officials who have information on local recycling resources—who can answer specific questions about recycling and waste management in your city or town. Look in your phone book under "Recycling Coordinators," or contact the relevant city or county government office (often called Department of Sanitation or Department of Public Works). Your state Department of Environmental

Protection or Department of Natural Resources also may have helpful resources.

- **Paper:** Newspaper is almost always recovered in community recycling programmes. Some communities also collect white and coloured paper (sometimes combined as 'mixed paper') and used cardboard boxes, such as cereal boxes.
- **Plastics:** Not all communities recycle all types of plastic. Investigate your community's plastic collection through the resources listed above. Most communities recycle plastic items such as detergent bottles, beverage containers (*e.g.*, soda, milk, and juice), and containers for various household products, from shampoo, lotion, and mouthwash containers to plastic peanut butter containers. Also, many grocery stores collect used plastic grocery bags on site for recycling.
- **Aluminum:** Almost all recycling programmes include aluminum beverage cans One of the most highly recycled products, aluminum cans are made into new cans in as little as 90 days after they are collected. Some communities also collect aluminum foil for recycling.
- **Steel:** Many steel products manufactured in the United States contain a high percentage of recycled steel. Some are even made from 100 per cent recycled steel. Many communities collect soup cans and other steel food packaging containers, as well as steel aerosol cans, for recycling.
- **Glass:** Glass food containers, such as jars and bottles for pickles, juice, jam, or wine, are usually recyclable in many communities.
- **Yard Trimmings/Food Scraps:** Many.communities have regular or seasonal programmes in place to collect yard trimmings, such as leaves, branches, and grass clippings, from residents. Other communities encourage residents to practice backyard composting for yard trimmings and food scraps.

• How can I start a recycling/composting programme in my community?

Starting a local recycling programme might not be as tough as you think. Your first step should be to get in touch with the proper authorities in your area. Most communities have recycling coordinators—government officials who have information on local recycling resources. Look in your phone book under 'recycling coordinators' or contact your local Department of Public Works or Department of Sanitation.

Everyone knows that reducing waste is good for the environment because it conserves natural resources. What many people don't know is that solid waste reduction and recycling also have an impact on global climate change.

The manufacture, distribution, and use of products—as well as management of the resulting waste-all result in greenhouse gas emissions. Greenhouse gases, which trap heat in the upper atmosphere, occur naturally and help create climates that sustain life on our planet. Increased concentrations of these gases can contribute to rising global temperatures, sea level changes, and other climate changes.

Waste prevention and recycling-jointly referred to as waste reduction-help us better manage the solid waste we generate. But reducing waste is a potent strategy for reducing greenhouse gases because it can:

- ***Reduce emissions from energy consumption:*** Recycling saves energy. Manufacturing goods from recycled materials typically requires less energy than producing goods from virgin materials. When people reuse goods or when products are made with less material, less energy is needed to extract, transport, and process raw materials and to manufacture products. When energy demand decreases, fewer fossil fuels are burned and less carbon dioxide is emitted into the atmosphere.
- ***Reduce emissions from incinerators:*** Recycling and waste prevention divert materials from incinerators and thus reduce greenhouse gas emissions from waste combustion.
- ***Reduce methane emissions from landfills:*** Waste prevention and recycling (including composting) divert organic wastes from landfills, reducing the methane that would be released if these materials decomposed in a landfill.
- ***Increase storage of carbon in forests:*** Trees absorb carbon dioxide from the atmosphere and store it in wood in a process called 'carbon sequestration.' Waste prevention and recycling paper products allows more trees to remain standing in the forest, where they can continue to remove carbon dioxide from the atmosphere.

• What happens to my recyclables after I put them out at the curbiside?

After you put your recyclables out on the curb, they begin a circular journey during which they are processed and manufactured into new recycled-content products, which are sold in stores to consumers, who can then repeat the process. Below is a brief summary of the three phases of the recycling loop.

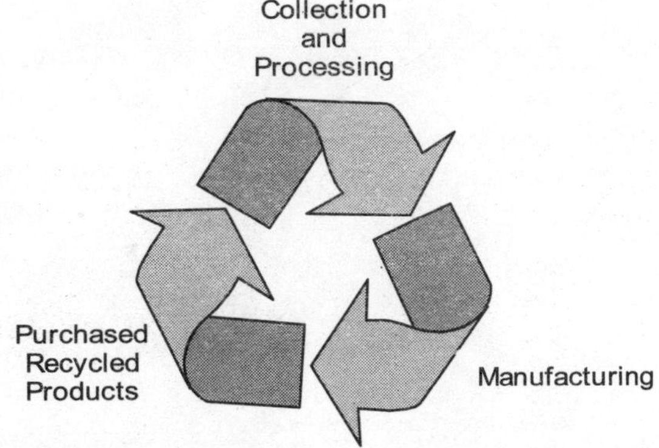

Step 1. Cotteetion and Processing: After recyclables are collected at the curb or from a drop-off centre, haulers take them to a materials recovery facility, where they are sorted and baled.

Step 2. Manufacturing: Once they are cleaned, separated, and baled, recyclables are remanufactured into new products. Many consumer products, such as newspapers, aluminum and steel cans, plastic containers and other plastic products, and glass bottles, are now manufactured with total or partial recycled content.

Step 3. Purchasing Recycled Products: Purchasing recycled products completes the recycling loop. By 'buying recycled,' governments, businesses, and individual consumers each play an important role in making the recycling process a success.

Municipal Solid Wastes and Recycling

Solid Wastes

Litter along the roadsides, trash on the beaches, heaps of refuse in the streets, the pungent piles of rotting garbage are unpleasant reminders of untidy human habits. Thousands of backyards, vacant plots contain the remains of discarded machines, parts of vehicles, food wastes and so on. Open dumps scar the landscape. In some countries solid wastes are dumped into the ocean. The growing mass of solid waste produced annually the world over includes millions of tons of paper and paper products, plastics, billions of bottles, cans, tyres, junked machines and discarded automobiles and millions of other appliances of different sizes and kinds. Probably the United States produces the largest solid waste. The city of New York produces the largest waste around one tonne each household per year. Around 15 per cent of solid waste from every household in an affluent society consists of food wastes. There is considerable loss of raw material and energy which goes into the manufacturing of the material thrown away as solid waste.

Disposal of Solid Wastes

The most commonly used methods for final disposal of solid wastes are sanitary landfill and open dumping. These methods are cheaper than the other disposal methods. The other advantage is that we can avoid the acute pollution problems associated with discharging wastes into waterways or polluting the air from incineration.

If properly planned, landfills can be used later for construction sites or recreational facilities. However, there are major disadvantages to open dumps, which are a public health problem, breeding flies, rats etc. Burning combustible wastes produces mixtures of particulate and gaseous matter that are obnoxious. Land disposal of solid wastes requires large parts of land. The increasing demand of land for human habitations and the ever-growing mountain of solid waste make the problem complex.

The adverse economics of this type of the disposal of solid wastes are far-reaching. Mineral resources such as copper, zinc, lead and tin are limited, and the ores are non-renewable. These metals are not destroyed by disposal but are often scattered beyond recovery, The squandering of these resources that occur when wastes are dumped indiscriminately, will produce a disruptive economic impact at some time in the future unless improvements are adopted. *Recycling* will alleviate some problems associated with the increasing density of population.

Incineration

In most developed countries the residents collect the wastes in polythene bags, and put them at prescribed places at a certain time of the day. Then onwards it becomes the responsibility of the municpal or other local bodies to collect and carry them to appropriate disposal sites. In well organised waste disposal systems articles such as cans, bottles etc. are separated and then the remaining garbage subjected to compaction in special trucks. These are transported to selected garbage disposal sites, like landfills, composting pits, open dumps or to incinerators. Once the garbage is collected, useful or recycable articles are separated. In India, some people earn or their livelihood by selling renewable resources handipicked from garbage. The solid wastes to be incinerated are *highly combustible* trash, like paper, carboard, plastics or rubber scrap, *combustible* wastes like wood scraps, cartons, floor sweepings, food wastes and other combustible articles. The incinerators produce toxic ash which must be landfilled.

The incinerators are so designed that the heat generated during incineration may be usefully utilised. The most common use is to generate steam. This partly recovers the cost of waste collection and disposal. Some waste materials produce corrosive fumes. Hence a careful segregation of such materials is desirable before compaction and incineration.

Recycling

Recycling Through Composting

One of the best places to start recycling is in the home garden with a compost pile. Compost, by definition, represents a mixture of plant material, soil eggshells, straw, manure, and other materials that can be broken down by microrganisms (bacteria and fungi). Its main value for use in the home garden, after decomposition has converted it into rich humus, is to improve soil texture, increase soil water-holding capacity, serve as a much, prevent or related weed growth, and protect plants from excess winter injury due to low temperatures or desication. It may also serve as source of nutrients, especially if ashes and manure have been added to the compost pile. However, the fertilizer value of most compost humus is low; 0.5 per cent nitrogen, 0.4 per cent phosphorus, and 0.2 per cent potassium.

To make good humus we can add the following to a compost pile: eggshells, citrus rinds, coffee grounds, kitchen vegetable garbage, tops of cut perennials, leaves, grass clippings, weedy annuals, ashes, straw, manure, crushed granitie rock, soil, inorganic fertilizer, seaweed, overripe fruit, water, and earthworms.

Such a mixture of garden and home by-products will contain many types of fungi and bacteria which act to decompose the compost substrates. However, to make sure that decomposition occurs satisfactorily, many compost makers add *compost starter,* which is an aqueous suspension of bacteria and/ or fungi that are adept at breaking down vegetable matter. The decomposition action by these organisms works best under aerobic conditions in warmer weather where there is a favourable supply of moisture. Like secondary treatment of sewage, the microbial action breaks down the vegetable and other matter to humus plus CO_2 and, in the process, liberates much heat, generating temperatures typically between 50 and 80°C.

A compost pile may be senstructed in many ways but basically, one makes alternating layers of vegetable matter and soil. To simulate microbial action, some fertilizer and water should be added periodically to the compost pile, especially during periods when the air temperature is warm. The soil is primarily added to provide a source of microorgaisms and to hasten the microbial decomposition action by these microrganisms. It also retains moisture needed by these organisms to grow.

Energy Production Through Recycling

Another approach to recycling involves the use of animal wastes (manure) and plant debris (including algae) to produce methane (CH_4) and organic fertilizer for urban, farm, and garden use, Methane (biogas) generators are in widespread use in Germany, France, India, Japan and the United States. They can be used in both northern temperate and in tropical regions. Several of the big advantages to their use are that they utilize readily available substrate, they help to solve energy needs especially when used in combination with wind generators and solar panels; they provide useful fertilizer by products.

In contrast to composting, an aerobic operation, methane generators involve breakdown of organic matter in the absence of oxygen (anaerobic conditions). The latter, therefore, involves a well-known process called fermentation. The main products of this fermentation are CH_4 and CO_2, with trace amounts of hydrogen sulphide and nitrogen gas given off. The conversion occurs at or around normal atmospheric pressure and at temperatures ranging between 15 and 50°C.

In general, conversion of 450 g of dry organic matter yields between 4.5 to 6.5 cubic feet of methane. In India methane gas generators are called *biogas plants*.

Recycling Paper and Plastics

The United States recycles about one-fifth of its paper. In contrast, Japan recycles about one-half of its paper. Harvesting to make pulp for paper manufacture costs less than the recycling process. Removal of ink is now feasible but expensive, and recycled paper is generally not useful in making white bond or slick paper for magazines. Recycling will become more profitable as pulp becomes more scarcre, labour costs increase, and recycled paper comes into greater use.

One of the most emphatic arguments for recycling paper is that it results in a reduction of solid waste and a reduction of the demands placed on a nation's forests and woodlots. The rate at which timber is being cut in forests for lumber and pulp is indeed alarming.

Non-degradable plastics are put in disposal sites. They make a relatively stable material for landfil because they do not breakdown and pollute underground water systems. Some plastics are however degradable. In developing and under-developed countries plastics are generally recycled. However, the quality of recycled plastics is not as good.

Various methods have been devised to separate non-ferrous from ferrous metals; glass from metal and different colours of glass. Of course the more economical method of achieving this separation is in individual homes, restaurants and other places where the materials are used. Broken glass is used in the manufacture of more glass bottles. This saves energy—melted glass uses only 2/3rd of heat energy required to produce fresh glass from silica and lime. Metal is easily recycled. Used tyre casing are suitable for reuse in the manufacture of synthetic rubber. Shreaded tyres mixed with rubber-base stock is used for playground surfacing.

Developing Countries

The hi-tech methods used for solid waste management and sewage treatment are highly expensive and beyond the reach of developing nations. In most of these countries sewage is discharged untreated into open drains and then on to rivers or open seas. Some countries including India and Thailand use a low-tech system of sewage treatment. The first step of this system is the same as the hi-tech system. The liquid waste is then left in open pond for conversion of organic waste through photosynthesis. The low-tech system requires three times more space than the high-tech one. There are no programmes for solid-waste management. Most of solid waste is dumped on to open ground and used for landfil. Renewable resources like plastics, glass, metal etc. are however, recycled.

PROSPECTS FOR UTILIZATION OF MUNICIPAL SOLID WASTE (MSW) IN INDIA

Municipal solid waste generation in India is increasing day by day. The average per capita generation of waste was about 500 g/day in 2007 and it will increase to 925 g/day by 2047. The most important step to be used for management of this waste would be minimising its generation but this is not really possible. Then to manage waste sustainably, the waste to wealth route remains a viable solution although in India it is not common practice. Maximum recycling, composting with organic municipal solid waste and waste to energy generation should be utilised for MSW management. This approach of sutainable waste management can solve the problem of land required for waste disposal and resulting pollution problems of air, ground, surface water, soil etc.

India has second largest population in the world (16.7 per cent of the world population) and accounts for a meager and 2.4 per cent of the world surface area. With the changing pattern of life style and consumer economy waste generation is increasing rapidly in India and the annual municipal waste generation. (MSW) is 50 million tonnes/year (5 million tonnes/year is hazardous waste) already. This is estimate to increase to approximately 310 million tonne annually by 2047 (Table 7.1).

Table 7.1. Increase in Municipal Solid Waste in India

Years	1950	2000	2050
Uraban Population (millions)	57.8	256.0	—
Daily Per Capita Waste Generation (Grams)	300.0	550.0	1050
Total Waste Generated (Million tonnes)	7.0	56.0	330
Area Under Land Fills (Thousand of ha)	0.15	25.4	160
Annual Methane Emissions (million Tonnes)	1.25	10.2	58

Municiapl solid waste (MSW) generation is around 500 g/day/person. This is estimated to further increase to 925 g/capita/day by 2047. The MSW contains largely food/organic waste, papers, plastics textiles, rubber, leather, wood, glasses, batteries, ferrous and non-ferrous metals containing components etc. Indian MSW has 40-60 per cent of compostable material or organic material with high moisture contents (Table 7.2 and 7.3).

Table 7.2. Physcial Characteristics of MSW in Indian Cities

Population Range (in million)	No. of cities surveyed	Paper	Rubber, Leather and synthetics	Glass	Metals	Total Compostable metals	Inert
0.1 to 0.5	12	2.91	0.78	0.56	0.33	44.57	43.59
0.5 to 1.0	15	2.95	0.73	0.35	0.32	40.01	48.38
1.0 to 2.0	9	4.71	0.71	0.46	0.49	38.95	44.73
2.0 to 5.0	3	3.18	0.48	0.59	56.67	49.07	
>5	4	6.43	0.28	0.94	0.80	30.84	53.90

All values in % and are calculated on dry weight basis.
(*Source:* Manual on MSW management for GOI, Urban Development Ministry, 2000)

Table 7.3. Chemical Characteristics of MSW in Indian Cities

Population Range (in million)	No. of cities surveyed	Moisture %	Organic Matter	N as (TN)	P as P_2O_5	K as K_2O	C/N ratio	Calorific Value in K cal/Kg
0.1 to 0.5	12	25.18	37.09	0.71	0.63	0.82	30.94	100.89
0.5 to 1.0	15	23.52	25.14	0.66	0.56	0.69	21.13	900.61
1.0 to 2.0	9	26.98	26.89	0.64	0.82	0.72	23.68	980.05
2.0 to 5.0	3	21.03	25.06	0.56	0.69	0.78	22.45	907.45
>5	4	38.72	39.07	0.56	0.52	0.52	30.11	800.70

All Values except moisture are on dry weight basis.
(*Source:* Manual of MSW Management for GOI, Urban Development Ministry, 2000)

The rising inconie levels and in turn greater purchasing power of individuals especially in big cities have given rise to consumer preferences that make goods obsolete quickly and this has led to a sharp rise in minds of policy makers, regulators and concerned citizenry. One recent example of tragic impact of improper management of municipal solid waste was seen as epidemic in Surat, Gujarat in 1994. Land scarcity in the cities has made waste disposal more difficult. The use of landfill is no longer considered to be a satisfactory environmental solution due to many health hazards linked with it. Therefore, generation of wastes. Wastes pose a severe challenge for Municipal Authorities for its sound disposal and the problem has been agitating the new methods have to be found to produce wealth from the waste. Obviously, the impact on environment can be reduced by reducing waste generation itself and failing this, waste should be either recycled or reused. When these options are unsuitable, waste must be incinerated for energy recovery. The last resort should be used in landfills because it requires space and run the risk of leakage.

NATURE IMPACTS BY UNPLANNED DUMPING OF MSW

Some nature influences are ground water contamination through leachate generation, surface water contamination by run-off from waste dumps, fire menace, bird meance, bad odours from dumping sites, epidemic through stray animals, global warming due to release of greenhouse gases (methane and CO_2), acidification of surrounding soils, stratospheric ozone deletion, photo-oxidant formation, etc. These can be rid of if MSW is put to some use. It should be noted that much of MSW may be rich in nutrients.

Thus, it is need of the hour to bring technological interventions for achieveing waste reduction and its utilisation. Waste should be regarded as resource/wealth lying at a wrong place. Thus in view that it has immense potential for resource recovery, it is required that MSW is looked from cradle to grave, properly collected, kept transported segregated and made ready to be disposed. Only those wastes should be sent for dumping which cannot be reused or recycled. The organic waste can be used as compost. The approach in waste management should be such that maximum possible waste generated could be used in one way or the other.

Proper management of MSW requires sensitizing the community about the importance of environmentally sound waste management practices, as well as concerted efforts should be made for adoption of a scientific approach by the concerned authorities. The biggest challenge is to ensure that different kinds of wastes are stored and segregated from the very beginning when individuals or families reject them.

Waste to Wealth Potential

Decrease in waste generation should be the first priority in MSW management hierarchy and then comes its maximum recycling possiblities. The 3R principle Reduce, Reuse and Recylce should be used to minimize waste generation. Now there is a fourth R which implies Rebuy. Thus, encouraging to rebuy the products made from the recycling of MSW, recycling industries can be promoted. There is no process in the world which has zero or no waste generation.

Some of the steps that can be taken for waste to generate 'wealth' from MSW are as follows:

Municipal Solid Waste Composting

Composting of MSW is recognized as a cost-effective method for waste management that results in an end product that can be used as a soil conditioner with beneficial effects on soil productivity.

In India MSW has 40-60 per cent (or sometime more) of compostable material with high moisture contents. The high moisture contents and low calorific value makes it unsuitable for incineration. Biomethanation and composting are perhaps better alternatives for treatment of wastes.

Energy Generation from Waste

In the waste management hierarchy, waste to energy (WTE) has been considered as a mode for the recovery of resources that must be considered before ultimate disposal of the final inert materials.

It is a fact that incineration plants are expensive. Because of this reason burning technologies are considered as inappropriate method of waste management by environmentalists. Several incineration plants that were installed in Delhi and Lucknow have failed to deliver rated energy outputs and have since been closed. However, there have been success stories elsewhere and the Government of India provides subsidy for incinerаters of increaters which not only generate power but reduce the bulk of wastes to a small volume of ash.

Biomethanation Anaerobic Digestion

Methane is produced by anaerobic decomposition of landfill solid waste and it contributes towards global warming. Methane is 21 times more potent green house gas (GHG) than CO_2. Calorific value of landfill gases is app. 4500 Kcal/m^3. Biomethanation technique of using methane gas for combustion or electricity generation could also provide compost for soil conditioning. This technique can be effectively used in a developing country like India. The methane value estimated for wastes generated in six selected metropolitant cities in India is two million tonnes/annum to several times more. It is expected to increase to 39 million tonnes/annum by 2047.

Pelletisation of Refuse Derived Fuel (RDF)

This proven and tested technology has been widely implemented in Europe for disposal of MSW and this RDF is suitable for Indian cities. The pellets are a good coal substitute. The NOX and SO_2 emissions are less than what are emitted from coal burning and the calorific value of these pellets are 2500-3000 Kcal/kg. A 6.6 MW electricity generation plant from incinerated cellets is satisfactorily running at Mahboobnagar Hyderabad.

Incineration of MSW

Calorific value of MSW in India ranges from 600-1100 kcal/m^3 and 100 tons of raw solid waste can potentially produce 1-1.5 megawatt power. In Malaysia, where 80 per cent of MSW contains food, papers and plastics with 55 per cent of moisture contents incineration plants operate successfully. By incinerating 1500 tons of MSW day with an average of calorific value of 2200 Kcal/kg one can produce 640 kW/day[7]. In Delhi Municipal Corporation of Delhi (MCD) has planned to produce 16-20 MW of electricity by first converting MSW to RDF and then incinerating it to produce electricity.

Gasification Pyrolysis

This is a proccess of destructive distillation. In this process, MSW is heated to 900-1000°C so that pyroligenous liquid/water gas can be used in internal combustion engine to produce electricity. This is a bit expensive technique but can be used in more effective manner in small scale production of electricity.

VERMICOMPOST MAY BE USED AS A POTENTIAL BIOFERTILIZER

For sustainable development in agriculture, it is essential to improve the soil organic carbon status that has deteriorated under intensive chemical framing. Among the several bio-fertilizers, farmers may use vermicompost on account of its simple preparation technology, favourable climate support and easy availability raw materials. Farmers can use vermicompost by mixing with chemical fertilizers almost in every agro production for increasing the effectiveness of the chemical fertilizer. It performs better in floriculture, horticulture, houseplants, potting soil, fruits and vegetables productions. However, for any application, better result can be obtained if farmers apply the estimated amount after knowing its per cent of organic carbon and C: N ratio.

In spite of this remarkable achievement, recently, farmers are facing problems in harvesting crops for stagnant productivity and associated hazards of the technology. As it requires a huge amount of chemical fertilizer, pesticide, insecticide and even water, chemicals accumulate gradually into the soil that causes the deterioration of soil fertility and environmental quality. A review of over 300 published reports showed that most of the environmental impact indicators which have decreasing trends are floral diversity, faunal diversity, habital diversity, landscape, soil organic matter, soil biological activity, soil structure, soil erosion, nitrate leaching, pesticide residue. CO_2, N_2O, CH_3, NH_3, nutrient use, water use and energy use. However, organic farming system performed significantly better in all the above factors and performed worse in none. For eradicating these ill effects of modern agriculture, peasants are considering growing food without chemical fertilizers and pesticides throughout the world. Meanwhile, the global organic-food market has already crossed 31 billion US $ by 2005 with an average annual growth rate of 20-25 per cent. Though the production cost in the organic farming is slightly higher, yet it will be sustainable alternative on account of its biological, ecological and environmental supportive natural approaches. Government of India has already constituted a 'Task Force' to popularise the organic farming. According to the opinion of the task force, the application of organic manure is the only option to improve the soil organic carbon for sustenance of soil quality and future agricultural productivity.

Vermicompost as a Biofertilizer

Even earthworms that decompose the agricultural wastes naturally and supply organic manure in the form of cast, have also left from our fields now. Hence, the percentage of organic carbon in the harvested soil gradually decreases to such a minimum level that hampers the exchange of plant macronutrients. At this juncture we can reintroduce the earthworms into our field by preparing and using vermicast as a source of bio-fertilizer. It is biologically active mound containing thousands of bacteria, enzymes, remnants of plant materials and animal manures which were not digested by the earthworm. An important component of this dark mass is humus which is a complicated material formed during the breakdown of organic matter. It also provides many binding sites for plant nutrients *e.g.* calcium, iron, potassium, sulphur and phosphorous. It dissolves slowly rather than allowing immediate nutrient leaching. It has excellent soil structure, porosity, aeration and water retention capabilities, which can insulate plant roots from extreme temperatures, reduce erosion and control weeds.

Fig. 7.1 Preparation of Vermicompost by Women Folklores

Chemical Quality and Precautions

Casting contain five times the available nitrogen, seven times the available potash and 5.5 times more calcium than that found in 15 cm of good top soil. Moreover, vermicomposting adds valuable attributes *viz.* water retention, texture, nutrient availability and an ability to fight soil-borne plant disease like root rotten. In spite of these advantages, the use of vermicomposed either in pure or

Fig. 7.2.

mixed with chemical fertilizer as a farm manure, is still rare because the technology has not gone into farmers' concept. Aforesaid activists grop in 'Matar-Benay Trust' campus has been experimenting the use of vermicompost in different crop production for the last five years. Out of curiosity the author has collected eight different vermicompost samples from different farmers, farmers, co-operative and NGO's and estimated its percentage of carbon content and NPK values in *Shibaprasad Bandyopadhyay maati Parikshagar'* (soil testing laboratory) at 'Matar-Benay Trust campus, Hatsimul. Burdwan West Bengal. The results obtained are shown in the Table 7.4 below.

Table 7.4. Percentage of Different Macronutrients in Eight Vermicompost Samples

Sample	pH	% of Organic Carbon	% of Nitrogen	% of P_2O_5	% of K_2O
1.	6.60	3.83	0.40	0.074	0.301
2.	6.56	3.25	0.33	0.220	0.220
3.	6.54	2.66	0.27	0.160	0.280
4.	–	13.06	1.41	1.502	0.258
5.	7.22	15.30	1.60	0.405	0.960
6.	8.75	6.85	0.68	0.040	1.400
7.	8.53	3.64	0.36	0.100	0.570
8.	6.98	2.78	0.30	0.095	0.210

Table 7.4 reflects the estimated results of eight different vermicompost samples which show a very high variation of carbon content (2.66 to 15.3%) and also the percentage of nitrogen content in the vermicompost sample, which is obvious. But the problem is whether farmers know the percentage of carbon content and C:N ratio of the used vermicompost sample or not. Therefore, the nutrent content, particularly the C:N ratio of each vermicompost sample should be measured before applying it into the field even if the farmers themselves. Values of C:N ratio can be improved by using different animal manure as a feeding material to the earthworms, instead of using cow-dung only. In order to project this idea, some relevant data regarding the animal manure are shown in Table 7.5.

Table 7.5. Approximate Dry Matter and Fertilizer Nutrient Composition of Various Types of Animal Manure

Type of livestock	% of Dry matter	N	Nutrient	(kg ton^{-1} in raw waste)	
		NH_4–N	Total-N	P_2O_5	K_2O
Swine	18	2.72	4.54	4.08	3.63
Beef cattle	15	1.81	4.99	3.18	4.54
Dairy cattle	18	1.81	4.08	1.81	4.54
Poultry	45	11.79	14.97	21.77	15.42

Table 7.5 indicates that certainly the per cent carbon content, C:N ratio and NPK values of the vermicast will be higher by using the poultry litter as feeding material. This trend of higher NPK values is also reflected in the vermicast NPK values (Table 7.4). Intensive care is required for protecting the vermicompost pit from ant, birds, rat and direct sunlight. Shortly a large number of vermicompost products are coming into the market packed within beautiful containers without mentioning the percentage of organic matter and C:N ratio. Where as the farmers are now being advised to use vermicast as an organic manure to increase the effectiveness of the chemical fertilzer also, hence for the optimum benefit from the organic manure, information regarding bio-fertizer should be authenticated or verified thoroughly.

Vermicompost Application

It has been established that the earthworms are one of the most useful and active agents in introducing suitable chemical, physical and microbiological changes in the soil, thereby directly increasing the fertility of the soil. Vermicompost should be used, after checking its nutrient content and mixing with the chemical fertilizers in suitable proportions. Institute of National Organic Agriculture (INORA) has applied the vermicompost in different proportions with chemical fertilizer in sugarcane production at different places of Maharashtra, Gujarat and Karnataka. It has been established that 1:1 vermicompost and chemical fertilizer ratio is most effective in sugarcane production. In a certain region of New Zealand, grass production became doubled after introducing some European earthworm species. Researchers have shown that the mixture casting with peat moss at the ratio of 1:2, 2:1 and 3:1 performed better in all growth parameters of Marigold producition. They have also shown that earthworm casting increases the germination rate in seeding development of cucumber nicely. In Bangalore. India, earthworms successfully decomposed residuals from sugar factory and turned them into a soil nutrient which enabled 50 per cent reduction in the use of chemical fertilizer. Earthworm castings are the best imaginable potting soil for houseplants as well as gardening and farming. It can also be used as a planting soil for trees, vegetables, shrubs and flowers. It was also observed at the Matar-Benay' Thrust campus that vermicompost performed better in flowers, vegetables, fruits and nursery productions. It can also be used, by mixing with chemical fertilizers, in any agro-production for raising the effectiveness of the chemical fertilizer.

ELECTRONIC WASTE

In the past few years, technological advances in electronics have boosted the economy and improved the general lifestyle of a common man. The ever growing dependence on electronic products has paved the way for an emerging environment concern, called 'Electronic Waste'. Every year, an estimated 100 million computers and other electronic devices break or become obsolete and are discarded. Electronic waste, or e-waste, is an emerging problem as well as a business opportunity of increasing significance, given the volumes of e-waste being generated and the content of both toxic and valuable materials in them. E-waste is a popular informal name for electronic products nearing the end of their 'useful life'. Computers, televisions, VCRs, stereos, copiers, mobile phones and fax machines are common electronic products. Many of these products can be reused, refurbished or recycled. Unfortunately, electronic discards is one of the fastest growing segments of our nations waste stream. E-waste has become a problem of crisis proportions because of two reasons. Firstly, E-waste is hazardous as the vast amount of computers, televisions, mobile phones and other electronic products that are disposed of every year all contain a variety of toxic substances. When discarded electronics are dumped in landfills, or when the waste is incinerated, contaminants and toxic chemicals are generated and released into the ground or air risking pollution of the environment and toxins entering the food chain are astronomical. Another reason is E-waste being generated at an alarming rate, due to fast obsolescence along with rapidly evolving technology.

Constituents of E-Waste

Electronic and electrical equipment, consist of multiple components, some having toxic substances that can affect human health and environment, if not properly managed. Generally, these hazards occur on account of improper recycling and disposal methods adopted. There are number of harmful substances (metals) found in e-waste. *'Antimony'* is used primarily in flame proofing, paints, ceramics, alloys, electronics and rubber. Antimony is increasingly used as an alloy that greatly increases lead's hardness and strength. Its most important use is as a hardener in lead for storage batteries.

Antimony and its compound in small does cause headaches, dizziness and depression, while larger doses can cause violent and frequent vomiting *'Arsenic'* is found in small quantities in the form of gallium arsenide in light emitting diodes. Arsenic is a poisonous metallic element and chronic exposure to it can lead to skin diseases and lung cancer. *'Barium'* is a metallic element used in sparkplugs, fluorescent lamps and in vacuum tubes. It generates poisonous oxides in contact with air. Exposure to barium can lead to muscle weakness. liver and heart problems. *"Brominated Flame Retardants (BFRs)"* is used in the plastic housings of electronic equipment and in circuit boards to prevent flammability. More than 50 per cent of BFR usage in the electronics industry consists of tetrabromo-bis-phenol—(TBBPA). Ten per cent is polybrominated diphenyl ethers (PBDEs) and less than one per cent is polybrominated biphenyls (PBB). *'Beryllium'* found in power supply boxes contain cancer causing agent for lungs. *'Cadmium'* is present in rechargeable NiCd-batteries, CRT screens, printer inks and toners. Cadmium components, absorbed through respiration, seriously affect the kidneys. *'Chromium'*, found in data tapes and floppy disks, is used because of high conductivity and anti corrosive properties. Chromium (VI) compounds are irritating to eyes, skin and mucous membranes. It can also result in DNA damage. *'Lead'* is found in CRT screens, batteries and printed circuit boards. It is also used in solder, lead acid batteries, electronic components and cable sheathing. Exposure to high amount of lead can result in vomiting, diarrhoea, appetite loss, abdominal pain, constipation, fatigue and sleeplessness. *'Mercury'* is used extensively in fluorescent lamps, LCDs, alkaline batteries and mercury wetted switches. It is a toxic heavy metal, that bioaccumulates, causing brain and liver damage, if inhaled. Excessive exposure to *'Selenium'* used in photocopying machines, can cause selenosis, leading to hair loss, nail brittleness, and neurological abnormalities. *'Polyvinyl chloride'* PVC is an extensively used plastic in electronic appliances. PVC is harmful as it contains about 55 per cent chloride, which when burned gives rise to hydrogen chloride gas. This combines with water to produce hydrogen chloride gas. This combines with water to produce hydrochloric acid and if inhaled can lead to respiratory problems.

There are a number of valuable substances in electronic wastes Gold Silver, Aluminium plastic etc. are prestigious materials, which recyclers recover from e-waste. *'Silver'* is used mainly in connectors and PWBs to provide conductivity. In mobile phones, it is typically used in the electronics and keypad contracts in the elemental form. *'Gold'* is used in marginal amounts in connectors and PWBs. It is used to provide conductivity and connectivity. Gold has no harmful effects on environment and humans and it can be obtained again after recycling process. *'Aluminium'* is present in almost all electronic products in large quantities. It also provides conductivity. Its less cost, compared to gold and silver and because of its easy recyclability, aluminium is used extensively.

Disposal of E-Waste

The e-waste that is generated can be recycled, reused, and disposed off in landfills or incinerators. The reuse and recycling of outdated electronic products minimize the hazardous effects of electronic waste on the environment. Reuse and recycling also boost energy and resource conservation. After all possibilities for reuse have been exhausted and a computer is slated for disposal, is sent for recycling. By this it is meant that the old raw materials are reclaimed for use in making new products. However, the costs of recycling are still very high due to which most recyclers are not very much willing to take computers for recycling. If the waste cannot be even recycled then it is either sent to landfills or is burnt in incinerators.

Dumping waste into landfills contaminates the ground water and soil. Toxic chemicals in electronics products leach into the land over time or are released in the atmosphere. These toxic substances can migrate into ground waters, and eventually into lakes, streams, or wells, and raise a potential exposure to humans and other species by entering the food chain.

Burning electronic products into incinerators leads to the formation of toxic gases due to the presence of heavy metals such as lead, cadmium and mercury. Mercury released into the atmosphere can bioaccumulate in the food chain.

E-Waste and Industry

It is a proven fact that, all who produce, distribute, use and dispose of electronic products, have a moral responsibility towards managing electronic waste. Electronic equipment manufacturers should ensure that their products contain lesser toxic constituents, more recycled content and are designed for easy upgradation and disassembly. Initiatives have been taken by some leading companies in this regard.

- A new packaging technology is already in the offering at Anadigics, which will enhance its product's moisture sensitivity level.
- National Semiconductor reveals that most of its products are now lead free (except solder). It has also banned the use of cadmium, mercury and chromium in its products.
- Nokia has created a list of hazardous substance which will not be used in their products and has sent the same to its suppliers.
- The design of Hewlett-Packard's Office Jet 500 multi-purpose printer has elminated the need for plastic flame retardants by using a metal chasis and power supply enclosure, utilizes light-emitting diodes (LEDs) instead of a mercury lamp for the scanner, and eliminates the need for batteries by using flash memory technology.
- Apple's Macintosh Power Books have used longer-life, less toxic rechargeable lithium-ion batteries for the last three products generations, in place of nickel cadmium batteries.
- The primary plastic resin used in Intel's PCs and servers (ABS + Polycarbonate) have no flame retardants containing PBBs or PBDEs. None of their products contain asbestos, or include lead or cadmium as plastic additives.
- Panasonic is the first company to apply reflow type lead-free soldering to compact portable minidisc player PC boards. its video equipment division has been developing a low-cost tin-copper base solder.
- At Motorola, housings are made of standard engineering plastics. Several Motorola phone models have eliminated the use of brass inserts in their plastic housings.

Finding methods to keep electronic waste out of landfills is a challenge now for all the electronic product manufacturs, recycling and waste management organizations, government agencies and environment management organizations. Indian Government should draft legislation in this direction. If all consumers plan to phase out their obsolete computers and other electronic products at the same time, the country may face a tsunami of e-scrap. Ultimately, it is the balance of nature, which always holds supreme.

REFERENCES

Singhal, S., S. Pandey: *Teri Information Monitor on Environment Sciences.* 6.1: 1-4, (2001).

Messineo, A. and D. Panno: Municipal Waste Management in Sicily: Practices and Challenges. Waste Management doi: 10.1016/j.wasman.2007.05.003, (2007).

Chaya, W. and S. H. Gheewala: *Journal of Cleaner Production.* 15: 1463-1468, (2007).

Aggelides, S. M., P.A. Londra, *Bioresource Technology,* 71, 253-259, (2000).

Krishna, Gopal: Waste-to-energy or Waste-to-pollution?. 2005 http://www.infochangeindia.org/agenda5-14.jsp.

Government Bureau. Power Generation from Municipal Waste. (2007).

Rawat, M., K.U. Singh and K. A. Mishra, V. Subramanian: *Environment Monitoring and Assessment.* 137. 13, 67-74, (2008).

Kathirvale, S., MNM Yunus and K.S. Sopian, AH: *Renewable Energy.* 29. (559-567).

Basin, R. MCD Looks to Cash in on Biocompost Demand, *Times of India* 24 March p. 9. (2008).

Stolze, M., A. Piorr. A Haring and S. Dabbert, *Organic Farming in Europe: Economics and Policy,* University of Hohenheim. Hohentheim, Germany, (2000).

Prasad, R., *Current Sci.* 89. 252-254, (2005).

Ali, S.A., I. Khan and A.S. Ali, *Science Reporter,* 43, 1, 28-30, (2006).

Appelhof, M., *Worms Eat Garbage,* p.-68, (1982).

Lee, K. E., *Earthworms. Their Ecology and Relationship with Soils and Land Use.* New York: Academic Press, (1985).

Edwards, C. A. *Bio Cycle,* 36, 56-58, (1995).

Tisdale, S. L., W.L. Nelson, J. D. Beaton and J. L. Havlin, *Soil Fertility and Fertilizers,* 5th Edition p-598, Prentice Hall of India Pvt. Ltd. New Delhi-110001, (1995).

Joshi, N. V. and B. Kelkar, *Ind. J. Agril. Sci.* 22, 189-196, (1951).

Gaddie, R. E. and D. E. Douglas. *Scientific Earthworm Farming.* Vol. I, 175, (1975).

8

Hospital Waste Management

Introduction

The management of health care waste is a subject of considerable concern to public health and infection-control specialists, as well as the general public. It is a well-known fact that in several types of health care activites, various types of hazardous and contagious materials are generated. Even though the consequences of discarding such waste carelessly are well known, it is only recently that adequate initiatives to manage this waste in a scientific manner are being taken in India.

Unscientific disposal of health care waste may lead to the transmission of communicable diseases such as gastro-enteric infection, respiratory infections, spreading through air, water and direct human contact with blood and infectious body fluids. These could be responsible for transmission of hepatitis B, C, E and AIDS within the community. Health care professionals and the general public are at risk due to the diseases spread by improper treatment and disposal of waste. Rag-pickers expose themselves to disease like Hepatitis B, Tetanus, Staphylococci, etc. while handling items like needles, surgical gloves, blood bags etc.

What is Bio-medical Waste?

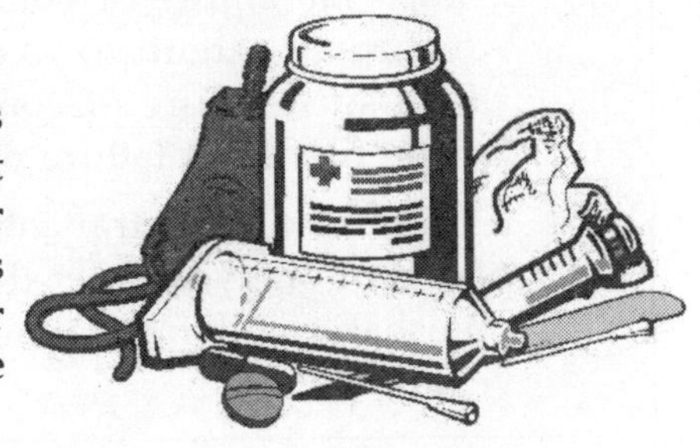

Bio-medical waste is "Any waste which is generated during the diagnosis, treatment or immunisation of human beings or animals or in any research activities pertaining thereto or in the production or testing of biologicals. It includes "any waste which is generated during the diagnosis, treatment or immunisation of human beings or animals or in any research activities pertaining thereto or in the production or testing of biologicals, and including categories mentioned in Schedule 1" as defined by the Bio-medical Waste (Management and Handling) Rules, 1998.

It includes infectious and non-infectious waste. Infectious waste includes pathological waste, cotton, dressing, used needles, syringes, scalpels, blades, glass, etc. and non-infectious waste includes general waste from the kitchen/ canteen, packaging material.

What are the Bio-medical Waste Rules?

The Government of India formulated the Bio-medical Waste (Handling and Management) Rules in 1998 (*hereafter referred to as the Bio-medical Waste Rules*) in order to specify procedures that have to be followed in the management and disposal of waste.

The Rules apply to all hospitals, nursing homes etc. in the country.

The Rules apply to all persons who generate, collect, receive, store, transport, treat, dispose or handle Bio-medical Waste in any form.

The Bio-medical Waste (Management and Handling) Rules; 1998 are conferred by section 6,8,25 of the Environment (Protection) Act, 1986 (29 of 1986).

Environment (Protection) Act, 1986

This Act is umbrella legislation providing a single focus in the country for the protection of Environment and seeks to plug the loopholes of earlier registration relating to environment. Several sets of rules relating to various aspects of management of hazardous chemical. Waste, microorganisms, bio-medical waste etc.

I. Whoever fails to comply with or contravenes any of the provision of this Act, or the rules made or order or directions issued there under, shall in respect of each such failure of contravention, be punishable with imprisonment for a term which may extend to one to five year or with fine which may extend to one lakh rupees, or with both, and in case the failure or contravention continues with additional fine which may extend to five thousand rupees for every day during which such failure or contravention continues after the conviction for the first such failure or contravention.

II. If the failure or contravention referred to in sub- section (*i*) continues period of one year after the date of convocation, the offend shall be punishable with imprisonment for a term which may extend to seven years.

The Act on Bio-medical waste management dated 27-07-98 puts the time limit to abide by all the specifications required for implementation as 31 December 2002. However, implementation of Bio-medical waste management is yet to be commenced in many places. One of the hurdles being posed is the low awareness within the health staff related to this topic.

Classification of Bio-medical Waste

Category	Description	Treatment & Disposal
1.	Human and Anatomical Waste Human Tissues, Organs, Body parts.	Incineration / Deep Burial.
2.	Animal Waste Animal Tissues, organs, body parts, carcasses, bleeding parts, fluid, blood and experimental animals used in research, waste generated by veterinary hospitals, colleges, discharge from hospitals and animal houses.	Incineration / Deep Burial.
3.	Microbiology and Biotechnology Waste from laboratory cultures, stocks or specimens of micro-organisms live or attenuated vaccines, human and animal cell cultures used in research and infectious agents from research and industrial laboratories, wastes from production of biologicals, toxins, dishes and devices used for transfer of cultures.	Incineration Autoclaving/ Microwaving.
4.	Waste Sharps Needles, syringes, scalpels, blades, glass, etc. that may cause punctures and cuts. This includes both used and unused sharps.	Disinfection Chemical disinfection / autoclaving / microwaving and mutilation / shredding.
5.	Discarded medicines and Cytotoxic drugs Waste comprising of outdated, contaminated and discarded medicines.	Incineration / Destruction and drugs disposal in secured landfills.
6.	Solid Waste Items contaminated with blood, and body-fluids including cotton, dressing, soiled plaster casts, lines, bedding, other material contaminated with blood.	Incineration Autoclaving/ Microwaving.
7.	Solid Waste: Items generated from disposable items other than sharps such as tubings, catheters, intravenous sets etc.	Disinfection by chemical treatment Autoclaving / Microwaving and Mutilation / shredding.
8.	Liquid Waste, Waste generated from laboratory and washing, cleaning, housekeeping, and disinfecting activities.	Disinfection by chemical treatment and discharge into drains.
9.	Incineration Ash, Ash from incineration of any Bio-medical Waste.	Disposal in Municipal Landfill.

...(Contd.)

10.	Chemical Waste Chemicals used in production of biologicals, chemicals used in disinfection, as insecticides, etc.	Chemical treatment and discharge into drains for liquids and secured landfill for solids.

Colour Coding and Type of Container for Disposal of Bio-medical Wastes

Colour Coding	Type of Container-I Waste Category	Treatment options as per Schedule I
Yellow	Plastic bag Cat. 1, Cat. 2, and Cat. 3, Cat. 6.	Incineration / Deep Burial
Red	Disinfected container/plastic bag Cat. 3, Cat. 6, Cat.7.	Autoclaving/Microwaving/ Chemical Treatment
Blue/White translucent	Plastic bag/puncture proof Cat. 4, Cat. 7. Container	Autoclaving/Microwaving / Chemical Treatment and destruction / Shredding
Black	Plastic bag Cat. 5 and Cat. 9 and Cat. 10. (solid)	Disposal in secured landfill

Bio-hazard Symbol

Bio-hazard symbol should be put up on all the coloured bins for segregation and the vehicles being used for transportation of Bio-medical Waste

How Do We Deal with the Waste?

Hospital waste is becoming increasingly complex due to changing technologies and increase in the services that the hospitals perform for the community. Management of waste presupposes a scientific approach to the process of waste generation, storage,- transport, treatment and its disposal. It is of utmost importance that bio-medical waste thus generated, be managed in an environmentally sound manner, which involves proper understanding of risks associated with the handling of such wastes. Only a cradle-to-grave approach will help in first minimizing, then collecting and finally treating and disposing the waste.

There are a few basic steps that hospitals have to follow in order to deal with Bio-medical Waste.

The first and the most crucial step being that of *SEGREGATION*. Segregation of waste refers to the basic separation of the different categories of waste generated (as given earlier) at the source of their generation.

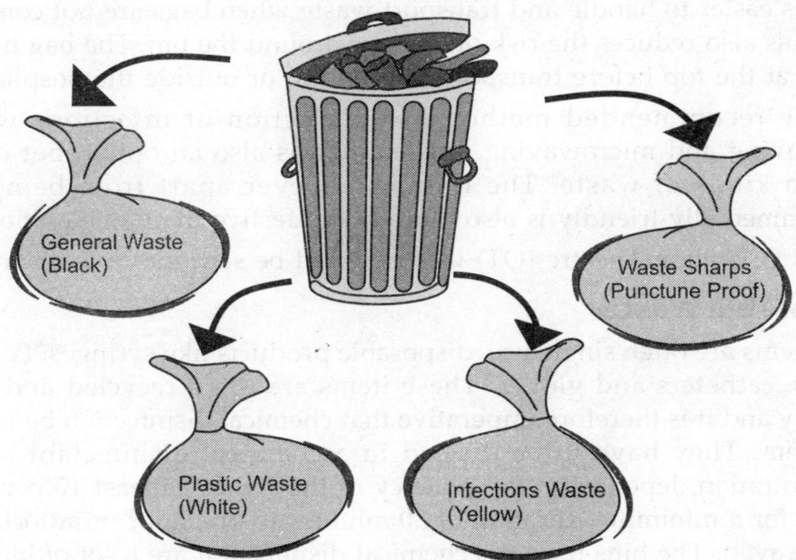

Treatment as per Colour Waste Category Schedule I of the Rules Code

The Bio-medical Waste (Management and Handling) Rules, 1998 have stipulated the following method of segregation on the basis of a simple colour-coded system:

How to Treat Waste?

Each kind of waste requires a different process of treatment depending on the material it is made of as well as the kind of micro organisms and waste it is likely to contain. Given below is a list of the different kinds of waste and the measures that have to be taken for safe handling and disposal of each kind of waste.

Infectious Waste

Bags should be colour coded and should also be properly labelled to avoid confusion while handling or disposing.

Infectious waste should be segregated at the point of generation itself and bins lined with inert material or with inner chambers for bleach should be used.

Usage of a lidded bin will discourage inadvertent use by others and also keep it away from the public.

Personnel involved in the handling of infectious waste should be provided with suitable protective gear. Proper training in managing this waste as well as in handing emergency situations like spillage of the waste should be given to them.

It is easier to handle and transport waste when bags are not completely full. This also reduces the risk of spillage around the bin. The bag has to be sealed at the top before transportation within or outside the hospital.

The recommended method of destruction of infectious waste if autoclaving and microwaving. Incineration is also an option but only for certain kinds of waste. The former however apart from being more environmentally friendly is also more cost effective than incineration.

All Operation Theatre (OT) waste should be sent for Autoclaving.

Disposable Waste

Such items are often single use, disposable products like syringes, IV bottles, sharps, catheters and gloves. These items are often recycled and reused illegally and it is therefore imperative that chemical disinfection be followed for them. They have to be dipped in a chemical disinfectant solution (concentration depends on the potency of the waste—atleast 10 per litre of water) for a minimum duration of 30 minutes to one hour or autoclaved or microwaved. The bins used for chemical disinfection are a set of bins—one inside the other. The smaller being perforated and easily extractable. This will help ensure that the bleach solution in the outer bin permeates the inner bin containing these waste items and minimises contact with the waste while the waste is being removed.

These items once disinfected have to be cut or mutilated in order to ensure that they are not reused. For instance, the fingers of the gloves should be cut and the IV bottles punctured.

Sharps should be handled with proper protection.

Blood bags should not be handled.

Bleach solution should be changed after every shift.

The plunger and the barrel of the syringe have to be separated before disinfecting it.

Sharps

Sharps as defined by the Central Pollution Control Board consist of needles, syringes, scalpels, blades, glass and so on. These are all capable of causing punctures, lacerations and cuts.

Sharps need separate attention as the risk of injury and infection by these is very high. They therefore have to be separated at the point of generation.

Manual bending, breaking or clipping of needles should be avoided as this may cause accidental innoculation. They should be destroyed with a Needle Cutter/Destroyer and then shredded.

Sharps should be placed in a puncture proof container and it has to be marked conspicuously by the Universal Bio-hazard symbol.

Liquid Waste

Liquid chemical waste has to be neutralised with reagents before disposal.

Liquid pathological waste has to be treated with disinfectant before disposal.

Treatment and Disposal of Segregated Wastes

- The segregated waste from all the bins (except Yellow bin) should be treated before disposal.
- The treated waste should be disposed off according to the categories.

The following table details how to treat the waste generated from each bin before it is disposed.

Sectons	Black bins	Red bins	Yellow bins	Blue bins/white puncture proof polybag or bin
Observation & LR	Medicine foil, medicine pocket, Spoiled mediciens	Gauze, Swabs, blood stained cotton, blood stained cloths, sanitary pad	Placenta	Needles, syringes, Urobag, Gloves, broken bottles, IV set, IV bottles, Catheters, Blood transfusion bag, mucus extractor, enema set,venflon.
Post natal & other wards	Medicine foil, medicine packet, Spoiled mediciens, food packets, plasteic carry bags, fruit peels waste food items, paper cups	Gauze, Swabs, blood stained cotton, blood stained clothes, sanitary pad, baby nappies, pus stained gauze	Umbilical cord shedding	Needles, syringes, Urobag, Blood transfusion bag, broken bottles, IV set, IV bottles, Catheters, mucus extractor, cord clamp, enema set, venflon.
Dressing room and Injection room	Medicine foil medicine packets, Spoiled medicines, paper cups.	Gauze, Swabs blood stained cotton, blood, stained clothes, Plaster, pus stained gauze	Tissues,	Needles, syringes Gloves broken bottles,
Laboratory	Laboratory Reagents, paper cups.	Gauze, Swabs blood stained cotton, Blood, urine, stool, sputum sample, used uristiks, pus stained gauze	Biopsy material,	Needles, syringes broken bottles, Tubes, pipette, glass slides, iancets
Store	Paper, medicine foils, packing material, expired medicine, paper cups.			Broken injection vials, medicien bottles, pre-sterilised disposable items where the packaging is tampered.

Deep Burial Pit

Deep Burial Pit for disposal of Human and Animal waste is the practical solution and has the approval from the Ministry of Environment and Central Pollution Committee for the rural areas and Towns where the population does not exceed 5 lakh and there is no Common Waste Treatment Facility available in the vicinity. The specification of the pit as per the figure given hereunder:

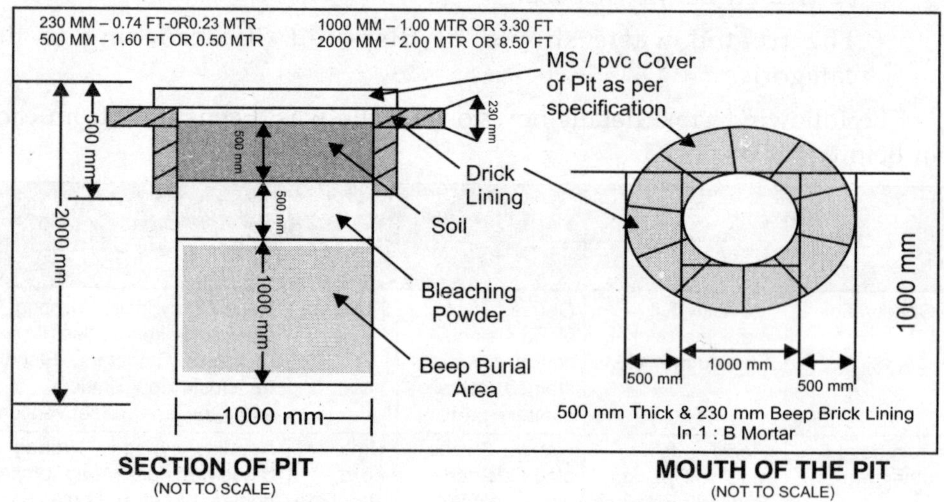

Deep Burial Pit Specification

1. A pit or trench should be dug about 2 metre deep. It should be half filled with waste then covered with lime within 50 cm of the surface, before filling the rest of the pit with soil.
2. It must be ensured that animals do not have any access to burial sites. Covers of galvanized iron/wire meshes may be used.
3. On each occasion, when wastes are added to the pit, a layer of 10 cm of lime powder and soil shall be added to cover the wastes.
4. Burial must be performed under close supervision.
5. The deep burial site should be relatively impermeable and no shallow well should be close to the site.
6. The pits should be distant from habitation, and sited so as to ensure that no contamination occurs of any surface water or ground water. The area should not be prone to flooding or erosion.
7. The location of the deep burial site te be authorised by the prescribed authority.
8. The institution shall maintain a record of all waste for deep burial.

Emergency Situations

Accidents should be avoided and therefore have systems to deal with emergency situations should be developed. One of the most common occurrences while dealing with Bio-Medical Waste is the spillage and leakage of waste.

Spill Protocol is therefore essential for any hospital. This refers to the measures that have to be taken to contain and decontaminate the accident site. This should include the following:

1. The surface containing the spill has to be mopped up with a swab soaked in disinfectant and then the swab should be put in the infectious waste bin.
2. No reagents should be sucked into the pipette with the mouth.
3. Other precautions to be kept in mind are the same as those followed in the rest of breathe-in the hospital.
4. Laboratories should be well ventilated so as to ensure that personnel do not breathe in contaminated air. Precautions should also be taken to ensure that the general public does not breathe in this air.

CENTRALISED FACILITY FOR BIO-MEDICAL WASTE

[Common Waste Treatment Facility (CWTF)]

- Small Healthcare Units, like Nursing Homes and Clinics, with minimal investment and space constraints may find it difficult to afford an individual disposal facility for bio-medical waste.
- In such cases these units could overcome this shortcomings by teaming up to establish a centralised facility for disposing off bio-medical waste.
- The Bio-medical Waste Rules also have provisions for such combined facilities.
- Many municipalities and corporations across the country are proposing to establish such common treatment facilities.

Community's Role in Bio-medical Waste Management

While management of bio-medical waste is primarily the responsibility of medical institutions and those who actually generate this waste, the community has a very important role to play in ensuring that the hospital practices the prescribed procedures for treating bio-medical waste.

Patients, who form a part of the community, constantly utilise services of healthcare institutions and hence they also share the responsibility of ensuring that these institutions do not pollute the community.

A community can therefore do the following to ensure a higher level of health:

- Communities should strive to ensure that awareness programmes should be conducted in their areas through residents' associations on the issue.
- Communities should ensure medical practitioners having clinics in their localities do not dispose off their waste in the municipal waste stream, but arrange to send it to the centralised facility.
- Communities should remain vigilant and should promptly report breach in proper bio-medical waste practices by any hospital to the pollution control board.

Patients Role in a Hospital

- Patients can ensure that they dispose off of waste only in the bins provided in the hospital and help keep the premises clean and litter-free.
- Patients should understand the system of Bio-Medical Waste Management followed in the hospital.
- Patients should make sure that they report any irregularities in the hospital to the management.
- Patients with infectious diseases should ensure that they strictly adhere to the procedure suggested by the doctors for disposal of body fluids like sputum.

Procedural Requirements under the Bio-medical Waste Rules

- Hospitals are required to file Form I to the prescribed authority for grant of Authorisation accompanied with the payment of the fee as prescribed by the State or Central Government.
- They are also required to submit a copy of their Annual Reports to the prescribed authority under Form II by January 31st every year.
- These reports shall be sent to the Central Pollution Control Board by the state pollution control board.

- ◆ Hospitals are mandatorily required to maintain records and report accidents under form III.

Overview of Technology used for Bio-medical Waste Treatment and Disposal

As bio-medical is a specialised class of waste, that is highly infectious and hazardous, there are specific technologies are required to treat and dispose the waste. The standard technologies being utilised in the country for treatment and disposal of bio-medical waste are:

- ◆ Microwave
- ◆ Autoclave
- ◆ Incineration.

Microwave

- ◆ The microwave is based on the principle of generation of high frequency waves.
- ◆ These waves causes the particles within the waste material to vibrate.
- ◆ Generating heat.
- ◆ This heat generated from within, kills all pathogens.

Autoclave

The autoclave operates on the principal of standard pressure cooker

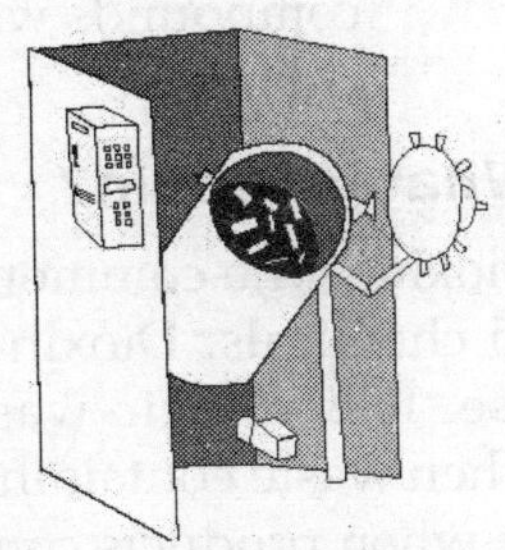

- ◆ The process involves using steam at high temperatures.
- ◆ The steam generated at high temperature penetrates waste material and kills all the micro organisms.

Incineration

A process that works on the simple principle of burning or combustion is technically called incineration. The incinerator, as the machine is referred to, uses either oil or electricity to power itself. Waste material is fed into the incinerator and is burnt in it. Normally incinerators are operated at temperatures between 300°C to 1100°C based on the volume of waste, the type of incinerator and the type of fuel used. Incinerators used in India are either single chambered or double chambered.

Incineration not only attempts to both kill the pathogens but also destroy the materials in which these reside - most of which are plastic disposables or cellulose rich materials etc. The burning of plastics, especially in unregulated incinerators is extremely hazardous as it creates a new set of chemical toxins, some of which according to current research, are highly toxic even in trace quantities. Some of the *chemical toxins produced by waste incinerators* are:

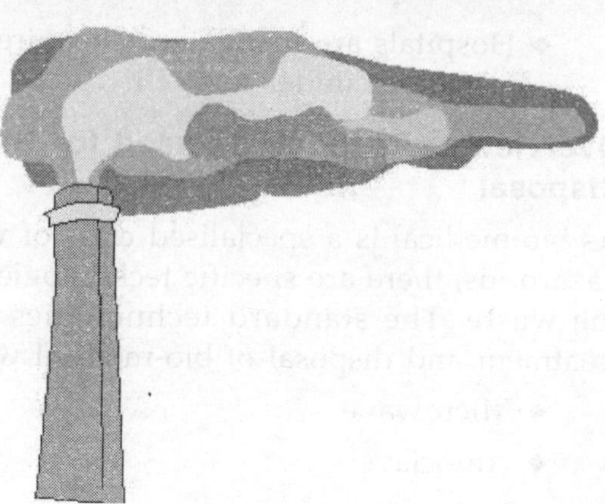

(*a*) Heavy metals, such as lead, cadmium, arsenic, chromium, nickel and so on, which are compounds that are present in plastics.

(*b*) Acid gases such as sulphur gases, hydrogen chloride and nitrogenous gases, particulate matter

(*c*) Dioxins and furans.

(*d*) Poly-Chlorinated Bi phenyls (PCBs) which, if not trapped in pollution control devices, have grave health effects on humans like endrocrinal problems thus causing disruptions in the human nervous system. If trapped, they become a part of the fly ash which is also very toxic and has to be disposed off carefully. Of these, *dioxins and furans are extremely toxic.* These belong to a family of polycyclic aromatic hydrocarbons compounds which are formed when PVC plastic present in the waste is burned.

What is Dioxin?

Dioxin is the common name for a class of 75 chemicals. Dioxin has no commercial use. It is a toxic waste product formed when waste containing chlorine is burned or when products containing chlorine are manufactured. PVC (polyvinyl chloride) plastic is a major source of the chlorine in medical waste. Commonly used PVC items in health care include medical equipment such as IV bags, gloves, tubing, oxygen tents, mattress covers, packaging and office supplies such as medical binders.

Exposure

When medical facilities burn their waste containing chlorinated plastics like PVC, dioxin will be emitted from the smokestacks of the incinerator. Dioxin particles travel long distances (transboundary). They are highly stable and do not break down and hence travel up the food chain. Ninety per cent of human exposure to dioxin occurs through our diets of meat, dairy products, eggs and fish. Dioxin builds up in fatty tissue.

Health Effects

Dioxin is proved to be a human carcinogen by the International Agency for Research on Cancer (IARC). Immune system disruption, reproductive and development Effects and hormone disruption are amongst the major health problems reported from dioxin exposure.

Incinerators are difficult to run : In hospital environments, technologies like incineration fail because untrained hospital staff operate incinerators. Surveys show that most Incinerators (over 85%) are operated at incorrect temperatures, do not destroy the waste completely, are fuel inefficient, and are out of order most of the time. There is a lot of difference between the theory and practices employed in the operation of Incinerators, making them a high risk method of disposal of waste especially medical waste.

Sources of Bio-medical Waste

The primary sources of Bio-Medical Waste are—Hospitals, Diagnostic Centres, Laboratories, Blood Banks, Nursing Homes and Clinics and Veterinary Hospitals and Clinics.

Non-infectious waste forms nearly 90 per cent of the waste generated by a hospital.

The remaining 10 per cent comprises of infectious waste and is generated in all the Wards, Operation Theatres, Intensive Care Units, Laboratories and Blood Banks. The waste generated in each of these areas can be categorised as follows:

- **General ward (Out Patient Department—OPD), Department wards, Intensive Care Unit and Emergency Care:** Cotton, dressing, bandages, syringes, needles, IV sets and tubing, blood sets, urine bags all contaminated with blood, pus or other body fluids and other waste like packaging, paper waste and food waste.
- **Operation Theatres:** Pathological waste, Cotton, dressing, instruments, contaminated plastic waste like syringes, tubing, IV sets, Blood sets, contaminated linen, contaminated gloves, caps, masks, hospital gowns used by the patients as well as the staff and doctors.
- **Laboratories:** Contaminated samples, cultures, pipettes, petridishes, tips, test tubes (both plastic and glass), slides.
- **Blood Banks :** Contaminated samples, cultures, pipettes, petridishes, tips, test tubes (both plastic and glass), slides, blood bags, unused blood bags (past the expiry date) and infected blood bags.

- **Nursing Homes and Clinics:** These generate the same kind of waste that hospitals generate but on a smaller scale depending on the facilities provided and the number of beds.

Why Bother about Bio-medical Waste?

- Such waste is hazardous to health care worker, rag pickers, and municipal workers
- Polyvinyl chloride and disposable medical supplies of plastics can be reused
- Incineration of PVC generates dioxins toxic to humans and environment
- HCW are at heightened risk because of frequent handling and exposures

Occupational Hazards

- Hospital staff and waste handlers in the hospital run the highest risk of contacting disease from following improper Bio Medical Waste Management practices as they are exposed to a multitude of diseases and infection. Therefore, in the interests of the hospital, recognising the importance of Bio Medical Waste Management at the earliest is crucial as apart from contacting disease, hospital staff can also be carriers of disease and infection.
- The current situation prevalent among healthcare waste handlers in hospitals is tantamount to violation of the basic human right of just and favourable conditions of work, in particular the Right to safe and health working conditions but also that of basic Right to Life and security of person.
- The hazardous nature of health care waste may be due to one or more of the following characteristics:
  1. It contains infectious agents.
  2. It is genotoxic (waste with mutagenic, teratoxic or carcinogenic properties). This kind of waste includes - certain cytotoxic drugs (those drugs with the ability to kill or stop the growth of certain living cells), vomit, urine or faeces from patients treated with cytotoxic drugs, chemicals and radioactive materials.
  3. It contains toxic or hazardous chemicals or pharmaceuticals.
  4. It is radioactive.
  5. It contains Sharps.

Infectious waste may contain a wide variety of pathogenic micro-organisms. Pathogens in infectious waste may enter the body through a number of routes: Through a puncture, abrasion or a cut in the skin. Through the mucous membrane—By inhalation—By ingestion.

- There is a particular concern about infection with the Human Immuno-deficiency Virus (HIV) and Hepatitis viruses B and C for which there is strong evidence of transmission via health care waste. These viruses are generally transmitted through injuries from syringe needles contaminated with human blood.
- Different pathogenic micro-organisms have varying abilities to survive in the environment. For example it has been found that the Hepatitis B virus is very persistent in dry air and can survive for several weeks on a surface; it is also resistant to brief exposure to boiling water. It can survive exposure to some antiseptic chemicals and remains viable for up to 10 hours at a temperature of 60° C.
- *Equipment that is essential for a worker handling waste:* Rubber gloves, shoes or boots, thick trousers and thick long-sleeved shirts. They should also be provided with convenient washing facilities (with warm water and soap) — particularly at the storage and incineration facilities.

  Periodic immunisation of hospital workers and staff against Hepatitis B is an absolute necessity.
- As far as cleaning up of spillages of body fluids or other potentially infectious waste is concerned, workers have to be provided with protection for eyes, respirators and hand tools like a shovel (to avoid direct contact with the waste) in addition to the standard gear mentioned above, in order to avoid any risk of eye injury and inhalation of any toxic fumes or dust.

Mercury in Hospitals

- Mercury is used in hospitals in thermometers, blood pressure instruments, feeding tubes, dilators and batteries, dental applications, fluorescent tubes and in specific laboratory chemicals. Mercury is a highly toxic metal that has the ability to pass all the four main human physiological barriers—skin, blood, brain and placenta. Mercury can cause a variety of diseases on exposure like-bronchitis, muscle tremors, irritability and personality changes. It can also affect the central nervous system in a variety of ways—impaired vision and hearing, paralysis, sleeplessness, emotional instability, developmental defects during foetal development and during childhood. It is particularly dangerous to foetuses, women of child-bearing age, pregnant women and young children.

  It is important to note that toxic heavy metals like mercury produce health effects and symptoms that are not specific and are common to other disorders. Hence, health effects of Mercury may be wrongly diagnosed or may even escape diagnosis *i.e.* they may not be attributed to heavy metal poisoning.

- Hospitals and health care service providers in western countries are switching to non-mercury alternatives and gradually phasing out mercury in medical applications. Non-mercury substitutes are not only safe but also more accurate than their mercury counterparts.

Duty of Occupier

According the Bio-medical Waste Management and Handling Rules — "It shall be the duty of every occupier of an institution generating bio-medical waste which includes a hospital, nursing home, clinic, dispensary, veterinary institution, animal house, pathological laboratory, blood bank by whatever name called to take all steps to ensure that such waste is handled without any adverse effect to human health and the environment".

A Cause of Concern

The major portion of Bio-medical Waste is generated in Hospitals and Health Care facilities where a good number. of patients visit with a hope of getting cured but if the Bio-medical Waste is not handled or managed properly, not only the patients will get further infected and acquire more grievous diseases than the ones they came to get cured of and even the attendants and the health care providers in these facilities are at equal risk.

Need of the Hour

Bio-medical Waste Management has been "Nobody's business" whereas it should be "Everybody's Concern".

There is need for a good coordination between the Management of Health Care providers and the Enforcement agencies (Pollution Control Boards) and then only the suggestions provided in the Environment Protection Act will get implemented.

There is big gap between enforcers and the implementers. The enforcing agencies should understand their role in a better way and should start facilitating the Health Care Providers to make administrative and financial provisions in their annual Plans. Efforts should also be made towards training the Staff at Hospitals and Clinics on the Bio-medical Waste Management.

There is also a great need to create a public awareness on the subject so that the community at large understands the risks involved.

REFERENCES

APHA Standard Methods for the Examination of Water and Waste Water. Editied by Andrew D. Eaton, Lenore S. clesceri, Arnold E. Greeberg 19th edition (1995).

Arion *et al.*, Hospital Solid Waste Management, A Case Study, J. Env. Engg. Div., 106 (EE4) August: 741-756 (1980).

Bio-medical Waste (Management and Handling) Rules, 1998 vide S.O. 630 (E) Ministry of Environment and Forest Notification, dated 20th July (1998).

HCOHSA, *Report of the Result of the Bio-medical Waste Management Survey*. Health Care Occupational Health and Safety Association, Toronto and Ontario Hospital Association, Onatrio (1985).

McGate, A.M. *Solid Waste Incineration and Heat Recovery at Royal Jubilees Hospital* B.C. Toronto (1980).

NEERI, *Manual on Water and Waste Water Analysis*, Nagpur, India (1986).

Government of India, *The Environmental (Protection) Act*, Gazette Vide S.O. 756 (E) (1986).

Tolerance Limits for Industrial Effluent Discharged the Inland Surface Water, Bureau of Indian Standards, IS: 2490 (1974).

Witts, *Information on Science and Technology Application Part-4*, Waterfalls Institure of New Delhi (2004).

Plastic Waste Management

Introduction

The plastics a marvel of polymer chemistry have become omni present in our daily life through various applications. But indiscriminate use of plastics as well as its reprocessing and disposal plastics waste are posing environmental problems and health hazards beside causing public nuisance.

The quantum of solid waste is ever increasing due to increased in population, development activities, and change in life style and socio-economic conditions. Plastics waste is as significant portion of the total municipal solid waste (MSW). It is estimated that approximately 10 thousands tons per day (TDP) of plastic waste is generated *i.e.* 9 per cent of 1.20 lacs TPD of MSW in the country. The plastic waste constitutes two major category of plastics: (1) Thermoplastics; (2) Thermoset plastics. Thermoplastics constitute 80 per cent and thermoset constitutes approximately 20 per cent of the total post-consumer plastics waste generated in India. The thermoplastics are recyclable plastics, which include polyethene terephthalate (PVC) high density poly ethylene (HDFE), poly propylene (PP), poly styrene (PS) etc. However, thermoset plastics; contain alkyd, epoxy, ester, melamine formaldehyde, poly urethane, metalized and multi layer plastics etc. The environmental hazards due I to mismanage of plastics waste include the following aspects:

(*i*) Uttered plastics spoils beauty of the city and choke drains and make important public places dirty;

(*ii*) Garbage containing plastics, when burnt may cause air pollution by emitting polluting gases;

(*iii*) Garbage mixed with plastics interferes in the waste processing facilities and may air cause problems in land fill operations;

(*iv*) Recycling industries operating in non-conforming areas are posing unhygienic problems to environment.

Recycled Plastics Manufacture and Usage Rules

Regulation of plastics waste, particularly manufacture and use of recycled plastics carry bags and containers is being regulated in the country as per Recycled Plastics Manufacture and Usage Rules, 1999 and as amended in 2003. According to these Rules:

- No person shall manufacture, stock, distribute or sell carry bags made of virgin or recycled plastic bags which are less than 8 × 12 inches in size and having thickness less than 20 microns;
- No vendor shall use carry bags/containers made of recycled plastics for storing, carrying, dispensing or packaging of food stuffs;
- Carry bags and containers made of recycled plastics and used for purposes other than storing and packaging food stuffs shall be manufactured using pigments and colourants as per IS 9833.198 entitled "List of pigments and colourants for use in plastics in contact with food stuffs, pharmaceuticals and drinking water";
- Recycling of plastics shall be undertaken strictly in accordance with the Bureau of Indian Standard specification IS 14534:1998 entitled "The Guidelines for Recycling of Plastics";
- Manufacturers of recycled plastic carry bags having printing facilities shall code/mark carry bags and containers as per Bureau of Indian Standard specification IS 14534: 1998 (The Guidelines for Recycling Plastics);
- No person shall manufacture carry bags or containers irrespective of size or weight unless the occupier of the unit has registered the unit with respective SPCB/PCC prior to the commencement of production;
- The prescribed authority for enforcement of the provisions of these rules related to manufacturing and recycling is SPCB in respect of States and the PCC in Union Territories and for relating to use collection, segregation, transportation and disposal shall be the District Collector/Deputy Commissioner of the concerned district.

Options for Plastic Waste Management

- **Recycling of plastics through environmentally sound manner:** Recycling of plastics should be carried in such a manner to minimize the pollution during the process and as a result to enhance the efficiency of the process and conserve the energy. Plastics recycling technologies have been divided into four general types—primary, secondary, tertiary and quaternary.

- **Primary** recycling involves processing of a waste /scrap plastics Into a product with characteristics similar to those of original product.
- **Secondary** recycling involves processing of waste/scrap plastics into materials that have characteristics different from those of original plastics product.
- **Tertiary** recycling involves the production of basic chemicals and fuels from plastics waste/scrap as part of the municipal waste stream or as a segregated waste.
- **Quaternary** recycling retrieves the energy content of waste/scrap plastics by burning/incineration. This process is not in use in India.

Steps Involved in the Recycling Process

- **Selection:** The Tecyclers/reprocessors have to select the waste/scrap which are suitable for recycling/reprocessing.
- **Segregation:** The plastics waste shall be segregated as per the Codes 1-7 mentioned in the BIS guidelines (1514534:1998)
- **Processing:** After selection and segregation of the pre-consumer waste (factory waste) shall be directly recycled. The post consumer waste (used plastic waste) shall be washed, shredded, agglomerated, extruded and granulated.
- **Use of Plastic waste in laying of Roads (Polymer Coated Bitumen Road):** The CPCB has undertaken a project in collaboration with Thiagarajar College of Engineering Madurai to evaluate the performance of polymer coated bi roads laid during 2002-2006 in different cities.

The observations are as below:

- The coating of plastics over aggregate improves Impact, Los Angels Abrasion and Crushing Value with the increase in the percentage plastics;
- The extracted bitumen showed almost near value for Marshall stability; The entire road was having good skid resistance and texture values;
- All the stretches in the roads have been found reasonably strong;
- The unevenness index values of these roods are nearly 3000 mm/km which indicate a good surface evenness;

- The plastic tar roads have not developed any potholes, rutting, raveling or edge flaw, even though these roads are more than four years of age;
- Polymer coated aggregate bitumen mix performs well compared polymer modified bitumen mix;
- Higher percentage of polymer coating improves the binding strength the mix;
- Foam plastics have better binding values.
- **Plastics waste disposal through Plasma Pyrolysis Technology (PPT):** Plasma Pyrolysis is a state of the art technology, which integrates the thermo chemical properties of plasma with the pyrolysis process. The intense versatile heat generation capabilities of PPT enable it to dispose off all types of plastic wastes including polymeric, bio-medical and hazardous waste in a safe and reliable manner.

Plasma Pyrolysis Technology

In plasma pyrolysis, firstly the plastics waste is fed into the primary chamber at 850°C through a feeder. The waste material dissociates into carbon monoxide, hydrogen, methane, higher hydrocarbons etc. Induced draft fan drains the pyrolysis gases as well as plastics waste into the secondary chamber, where these gases are combusted in the presence of excess air. The inflammable gases are ignited with high voltage spark. The secondary chamber temperature is maintained at around 1050°C. The hydrocarbon, carbon monoxide and hydrogen are combusted into safe carbon dioxide and water. The process conditions are maintained so that it eliminates the possibility of formation of toxic dioxins and furans molecules (in case of chlorinated waste). The conversion of organic waste into non-toxic gases (CO_2, H_2O) is more than 99 per cent. The extreme conditions of Plasma kill stable bacteria such as Bacillus stereothermophilus and Bacillus subtilis immediately. Segregation of the waste is not necessary, as very high temperatures ensure treatment of all types of waste without discrimination.

The CPCB has initiated the study in association with Facilitation Centre for industrial Plasma Technologies (FCIPT), Institute of Plasma Research (IPR) The objectives of the study are to conduct performance study of the PPT on 15 kg/hr prototype demonstration system developed by FCIPT/ IPR for proper disposal of plastics waste and also monitor air quality parameters *e.g.* suspended particulate matter (SPM), carbon monoxide (CO), hydrocarbons (HC), benzene, dioxins, furans etc. with regards to gaseous emissions. CPCB also proposes to undertake study on safe disposal of plastics waste using higher capacity (approx 50 kg/hr) plasma pyrolysis system as in future and may set up prototype plasma pyrolysis plant on demonstration basis (15 kg/hr waste disposal capacity) at specific locations (hilly and pilgrimage) in consultation with State Government.

Conversion of Plastics Waste into Liquid Fuel: A reasearch-cum-demostration plant was set up at Nagpur, Maharashtra for conversion of waste plastics into liquid fuel. The process adopted is based on random de-polymerization of waste plastics into liquid fuel in presence o catalyst. The entire process is undertaken in closed reactor vessel followed condensation, if required. Waste plastics while heating upto 270°C to 300°C convert into liquid-vapour state, which is collected in condensation chamber the form of liquid fuel while the tarry liquid waste is topped-down from heating reactor vessel. The organic gas is generated which is vented due lock of storage facility. However, the gas can be used in dual fuel dies generator set for generation of electricity. The process includes the steps shown ahead:

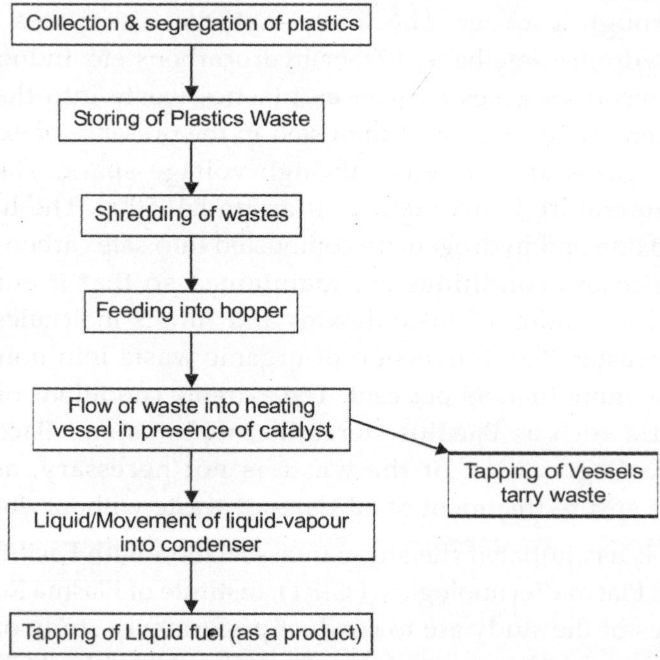

Environment Related Observations during the Process

- There are no liquid industrial effluents and no floor washings as it is a dry process.

- There are no organized stack and process emissions.
- Odour of volatile organics has been experienced in the processing area due to some leakages or lack of proper sealing.
- Absolute conversion of liquid-vapour was not possible into liquid, some portion of gas (about 20%) is connected to the generator. However, the process will be improved in full-scale plant.
- PVC plastics waste is not used and if used, it was less than one per cent. In case PVC is used, the chlorine can be converted into hydrochloric acid as a by-product.
- The charcoal (charcoal is formed due to tapping of tarry waste) generated during the process has been analysed and contain heavy metals, poly aromatic hydrocarbon (PAH) which appears to be hazardous in nature. The source of metals in charcoal could be due to the presence of additives in plastics and due to multilayer and laminated plastics.
- Monitoring of process fugitive emissions in the work area as well as emissions from the engines/diesel generator sets is necessarily required (where this liquid fuel is used) for various parameters such as CO, HCl, Styrene, Benzene, VOCs.

Biodegradable Plastics : The environmentally degradable polyolefin films are defined as those materials that contain degradation process of polyolefin article (bag/film/ sheet) under conditions of composting. Often queries are raised regarding biodegradability of plastics but clear-cut answer is not available about the biodegradability of plastics. In view of above, CPCB has initiated a study in collaboration with Central Institute of Plastics Engineering and Technology (CIPET) to establish the biodegradability and compostability (*e.g.* fragmentation rate, degradation role and safety) of polymeric material available in India and abroad. The study will include:

- Inventorisation and assessment of the manufacturing status of biodegradable plastics in India particularly with reference to processing technologies and the environmental issues.
- Establishment of the degradation rate (change in chemical structure, decrease in mechanical strength, fragmentation or weight loss) of the polymeric material plastics material under laboratory scale compos conditions.
- Finding out self-life and its impact on environment (soil, water plastics with reference to colour and additives, once it is disposed off).
- Assessment of effects on foodstuffs with reference to natural colours and additives.

Status of Plastics Waste Management in the Country

Central Pollution Control Board (CPCB) is co-ordinating with State Pollution Control Boards (SPCBs) and Pollution Control Committees (PCCs) regard to implementation of Plastics Manufacture and Usage (Amendment) Rules, 2003. The Prescribed Authorities for manufacturing and recycling plastics are SPCBs/PCCs whereas; Prescribed Authorities for segregation, transport and disposal of plastics waste are District Collectors/Deputy Commissioners. CPCB has compiled information relating to implementation of the said Rules and prepared status report on plastics w management (PWM).

State-wise Status of Plastics Manufacturing/Recycling Units (As December, 2006)

Sl. No.	SPCBs/UTs	No. of units	No. of Registration Granted	Comments/Suggestions
1	2	3	4	5
1.	Andhra Pradesh	177	177	The Plastics Manufacture and Usage Rules, 1999/2003 are being implemented. Levy of penalties against the violators of recycling norms are stipulated vide Notification No 25 dated 30.3.2001. The Board is encouraging urban local bodies to segregate waste at source so as to promote recycling. The Andhra Pradesh Pollution Control Board imposed a fine of Rs. 25.000/- each on 16 defaulting units and issued closure orders to 2 units during April 2006 to September 2006.
2.	Andaman & Nicobar Islands	Nil	Nil	Plastics Manufacture & Usage Rules republished by the Administration vide Notification No. 121 dated 5.5.2000. A committee was formed for effective implementations of the rules vide order No. 623 dated 23.7.2004. Administration is organizing regular awareness programmes
3.	Assam	10	Nil	Environmental Awareness programmes are being

....*(Contd.)*

1	2	3	4	5
				conducted regularly. Bi-lingual publications are brought out by the board regularly. The board is developing criteria for other plastics products such as ropes, sheets, soap case etc.
4.	Arunachal Pradesh	Nil	Nil	The Notification of the Ministry has been circulated to the concerned Department and Deputy Commissioner of the State for compliance by the State Government
5.	Bihar			Advertisements in local daily newspapers for compliance of plastic rules were issued. Inventory is being done. Offices of the State Board have been identified and notified to assist the District Administration for effective implementation of the rules
6.	Chandigarh	9	9if	The UT administration has notified the plastic rules vide Notification no. DC/M A/2001/ 187/dated 14.9.2001. Vide notification No. ED/2003/543 dated 16th September, 2003 the Government has restricted the thickness of plastic carry bags to be not below 30 microns and size not less than 8x12 inches
7.	Chhattisgarh	32	11	Inventorisation of plastic bag manufacturing units has been done. A committee has been formed to monitor the implementation of compliance. Awareness programmes are being organized from time to time by regional offices of the SPCB through media/ ecoclubs and NGOs etc
8.	Delhi	147	147	The Delhi Plastic bags (Manufacture, Sale and Usage and Non-bio-

....*(Contd.)*

1	2	3	4	5
				degradable Garbage Control Act, 2001 has been brought out vide DOE/2001 /Rules/451 dated 2-11-2001 to manage plastics waste. Vide notifications No. F.8 (86)/ EA/ Env. /2005(ii)/485, 486 dated 02.06.2005 & F.8 (86)/ EAIEnv./2005(ii)/450 on 25th May, 2006, the Government of Delhi has made the degradable plastic carry bags compulsory in all four and five star hotels, hospitals having bed strength of 100 beds and more and restaurants having sitting capacity of more than 50 seats, all fruits and vegetables outlets of mother diary, all liquor vends and all shopping malls. Public notices in Hindi and English newspapers about the plastic rules as well as management of the plastic wastes issued.
9.	Daman & Diu	-	-	The Notification of the Ministry republished on official gazette
10.	Dadara & Nagar Haveli	-	-	The Notification of the Ministry republished on official gazette
11.	Gujarat	200	94	Published public notices in Gujarati and English regarding RPMU rules, 1999 and its amendment in 2003. Gujarat Board has organized meetings at various levels to create awareness on plastics and the awareness programmes are organized periodically. The Board has completed the inventorisation. Government of Gujarat has banned the use of plastic carry bags at religious places *i.e.* at Ambaji, Dakar, Somnath and Dwarka

....(Contd.)

1	2	3	4	5
12.	Goa	125	17	The State of Goa has notified Goa Non-biodegradable Garbage (Control) Act, 1996. In this Act, the major implementer of this Rule is local authority, which has to provide various places/types of receptacles for deposit of "Non-biodegradable, Biodegradable and Biomedical" garbage/waste and also ensure that owners/occupiers of all lands and buildings abide by the regulations under the above said Act. Notification has been brought out and thickness of plastics carry bags for selling has been raised to 40 microns. Inventory on the units manufacturing carry bags / containers is in progress.
13.	Haryana	—	—	Plastics Manufacture & Usage Rules republished by the State. The SPCB has prepared inventory of 106 units so far and it has been reported that all these units are complying with the rules and they are manufacturing carry bags with more than 20 microns thickness.
14.	Himachal Pradesh	50	15(12)	The State has notified the Himachal Pradesh Non-biodegradable Garbage (Control) Act, 1995. Under this Act, the Government prohibits using coloured polythene carry bags manufactured from Recycled Plastics for packaging goods from 1st January 1999. Subsequently, in 2004, vide notification No. STE-A (3)-2/2003 dated' 4.6.2004 the Government imposed a ban on use of plastic carry bags of thickness below 70 microns and size less than 12x18 inches.

....*(Contd.)*

1	2	3	4	5
15.	Jharkhand	—	—	The compliance to the rules is being periodically monitored by the State Pollution Control Board. Rules disseminated through Public Notices.
16.	J & Kashmir	—	—	Plastics Manufacture & Usage Rules republished by the State Government.
17.	Karnataka	302	Nil	Public Notice issued 30.3.2000 & 7.12.2000. Municipalities are also involved in implementation of plastic rules. Reuse of plastics wastes are used in laying of Roads. Inter-state movement of substandard carry bags/ material etc. is restricted
18.	Kerala	193	10	Wide publicity has been given on the restrictions imposed as per Plastics manufacture and usage rules, 1999. State Government notified vide G.O. (P) N0.264/2003/LSGD dated 1.9.2003 prohibiting the plastic carry bags which are less than 40 microns in the State. Also the Govt. of Kerala has formulated an action plan for plastics waste management within the state.
19.	Lakshadweep	Nil	Nil	The administration imposed ban on packing and carrying of plastic bags for carrying consumer goods. Notification on "Lakshadweep Sanitation Conservancy Byelaws, 1998" was issued vide No. 17/2/96-ST&E dated 17.7.1998 to prohibit the use of non-biodegradable materials for packing and carrying consumer goods. Hoardings are displayed at prominent places indicating, "prohibiting littering of plastic waste". Awareness programmes are periodically conducted for phasing out plastic wastes.

....(Contd.)

1	2	3	4	5
20.	Madhya Pradesh	179	83	The State Government has issued orders dated 4.6.2003 declaring authorities for the implementation of the plastic rules as per the original notification. Board has organized wide publicity campaign regarding the provisions of the rules through various means like Articles in newspapers, workshops, leaflets, pamphlets, rallies exhibitions, TV and radio talks. Inventorisation is complete
21.	Maharashtra	—	—	Maharashtra plastic carry bags (Manufacture & Usage) Rules 2006 notified under Maharashtra Non-bio-degradable Garbage Control Ordinance 2006 published. Under these, the Govt. of Maharashtra has banned manufacturing of plastic bags below 50- micron thickness and size of 8x12 inches. Maharashtra State Pollution Control Board (MPCB) has taken actions against units, which are non compliant and also issued show-cause notices, directions and subsequent closures, if required
22.	Mizoram	Nil	Nil	Mass awareness campaign organized through publication, distribution of leaflets / pamphlets, by organizing radio, TV talks, seminars and discussions with NGOs and public.
23.	Meghalaya	1	Nil	The Meghalaya Prohibition of Manufacture, Sale, Use and Throwing of low-density plastic bags Act 2001 notified. As per this Act manufacture, sale, use and throwing of plastic bags less than 40 micron has been prohibited in

....(*Contd.*)

1	2	3	4	5
				the State. Authorities are designated by the Government for the proper implementation of the Rules.
24.	Manipur	—	—	Plastics Manufacture & Usage Rules republished by the State Government during June 2004. Monitoring on the compliance of the rules is being carried out by the State Pollution Control Board
25.	Nagaland	4	4	Plastics Manufacture & Usage Rules republished by the State Government vide notification no. GAB-9/26/2003 dated 12.11.2003 through which less than 20- micron poly carry bags are prohibited. The Board is also creating awareness on the eco friendly use of plastics through pamphlets etc.
26.	Orissa	14	2	Plastics Manufacture & Usage Rules republished by the State Government. Advertisement are given in the local newspapers to draw attention of the concerned for compliance of these rules. State level awareness programmes are being carried out regularly. Inventorisation of industries has been completed. In the State of Orissa, the use of plastic carry bags has been banned in the municipality area of Puri and Konark with effect from 01/04/2002
27.	Pondicherry	42	8	Pondicherry administration has republished the plastic rules vide G.O. Ms. No. 16/2003/Envt. Dated 1st December, 2003. Proposing to declare plastic free zone in the town. Also proposed a draft Pondicherry Non-bio degradable Garbage Control Act, 2003. Regular awareness drive is being created.

....(Contd.)

1	2	3	4	5
28.	Punjab	—	—	Usages of poly carry bags for foodstuff banned vide Order 8/21/STE (1)72221 dated 2.11.2000. Inventory of- the plastic manufacturing units completed. Punjab State Council for Science & Technology has introduced a Bill 'Punjab Plastic Carry Bags (Manufacture, Use & Disposal Control) Bill, 2004' which has been cleared by the State Government. This Bill prohibits plastic carry bags below 30 microns & size less than 8x12 inches and has got penalty provisions incorporated in it. Released public notices highlighting the salient features of the Rules in local newspapers for proper compliance. Board has organised several awareness meetings in various districts in the state.
29.	Rajasthan	—	—	Vide Circular No. 8(1) PLG799 1.6.2000 usage of poly carry bags for foodstuff banned.
30.	Sikkim	—	—	Usage of poly carry bags for foodstuff banned vide Sikkim Government Notification GOS/UD & HD/97-2000/6 (83)793 dated 30th March 2001. Regular awareness programmes are being conducted.
31.	Tamil Nadu	588	45	Massive awareness: drive initiated through publications in newspapers, programmes in TV and Radio, hoardings in prominent places and buses. Also a mobile awareness creations van is in operation. Inventory of manufacturing units completed

....*(Contd.)*

1	2	3	4	5
32.	Tripura	6	6	The manufacture, sale, distribution and use of virgin and recycled plastic bags and containers are prohibited vide Direction issued by Tripura SPCB dated 1 .9.2003. Board has issued number of advertisements in local newspapers to generate public awareness
33.	Uttar Pradesh			Usage of polythene carry bags for foodstuff banned. Non-biodegradable garbage control act notified vide No 2448 (2)/XVII-V-I dated 1- 11-2000
34.	Uttranchal	Nil	Nil	A draft of the Uttaranchal Plastic Bags (Manufacture, Sale and Usage) and Non-Biodegradable Garbage (Control) Act, 2004 has been prepared by the Board and has been sent to Government for notification. A task force has been created to organize mass awareness programmes. Published advertisements in the newspapers on plastic rules. Efficient collection of plastic waste for recycling is being organized.
35.	West Bengal	—	—	West Bengal Government is proposing a non- biodegradable garbage control bill. Plastics Rules Notified. The board has issued ban orders on the entry, use, sale of plastic carry bags in several heritage/tourist places. The West Bengal Plastic Carry Bags and Garbage Control Bill introduced in the State prohibit manufacture, Storage, transport and use of plastics made of recycled plastics. Thickness

....*(Contd.)*

1	2	3	4	5
				of plastic carry bags should not be less than 20 microns and for cups and tumblers are to be with 40 microns thickness. Board has published advertisements in the newspapers & organized awareness campaigns.

Strategy for Plastics Waste Management

Commonly littered plastic wastes include; polythene carry bags, plastic wrappings, thermocole packings, plastic plates, cups, spoons, glass, melamine crockery and other non-recyclable plastics waste such as guthka pouches, multi-layer packaging, laminated packagings etc. Estimated quantity of plastic waste is 5-10 per cent of total Municipal Solid Waste (1.2 lakh TPD) generation *i.e.* 6000 tons per day (TPD). It has been observed that in the present Rules, there are no provisions for the disposal of post consumer plastics waste. With the result, plastics waste is littered as road. The waste often chokes open drains as well as make the land infertile. Considering the ill effects and seriousness on the issue, following strategies are suggested to tackle the menace.

Issues of Concern	Strategy
Production of sub-standard plastic products.	Regulation of sub-standard plastic products.
Multilayer, laminated and thermoset plastic wastes are not recyclable.	Banning or alternate to non-recyclable plastic packaging.
Improper recycling without environmental consideration.	Improvement in recycling mechanism.
Improper regulatory mechanism.	Stringent action against defaulting units.
Inadequate and unsustainable plastic waste collection and disposal mechanism. (Only 50-60% thermoplastics plastic waste is recycled).	Promotion of alternate options for collection and disposal of plastic waste such as use in road construction, conversion into fuel oil, use in blast furnace/cement kilns, densification, balinge.

The Task Force

To formulate a strategy and an action programme for management of plastics waste, the Ministry of Environment and Forests constituted a Task Force comprising specialists, representatives of industry and civic authorities.

The Task Force in its report (August, 1997) recommended a package of preventive, promotional and mitigative (PPM) measures as also the *modus operandi* for their implementation. These include guidelines for compliance of environmental safety, specifications for restriction on recycling of poor quality plastics waste, deterrent penalties for littering, industry initiatives and collaboration with the civic authorities for improvement in plastics waste collection system, incentives for development and adoption of appropriate technologies and sustained campaigns for creating public awareness and involvement. Networking of concerned industry Associations, setting up of an Indian Centre for Plastics in Environment (ICPE) and constitution of an implementation and monitoring committee (IMC) were also suggested by the Task Force for follow-up of the recommendations. The task force has following object:

(*i*) To formulate a strategy and prepare an action programme for management of plastic waste;

(*ii*) To prepare incentives/penalties/levis for checking the growth of plastics packaging waste;

(*iii*) To prepare guidelines for packaging using plastics materials.

On the basis of the Task Force Report, several initiatives have been taken, while some are on the anvil. The Ministry of Environment and Forests has issued a Gazette notification prohibiting the use of recycled plastics for storing and carrying food staff. To restrict the indiscriminate use of plastic carry bags, the notification also stipulates the minimum thickness for such carry bags. Public awareness programmes have also been launched.

Plastics Waste Industry

The plastics waste industry has diversified its activities over the past 25 years. However, this diversification has not been accompanied with an appropriate body for plastics waste management in the country. The management of plastics wastes in India presents an interesting and economically feasible solution to the commonly labelled 'menace' of littering plastic wates in public places. The collection of plastic wastes is the source of livelihood for the innumerable 'rag pickers' or waste collectors who are followed by the kabadiwala and waste dealers. In most cases, an entire family is involved in this trade. Plastics waste collection is termed as a 'lucrative' business as against paper, cardboard, glass bottles and metal cans. A typical kabadiwala in Delhi displays the following rate list:

Newspapers in English	:	Rs. 4-5/kg
Newspapers in Hindi	:	Rs. 3-4/kg
Magazines	:	Rs. 3-3.50/kg
Iron/Loha	:	Rs. 5.50/Kg
Plastics Waste (mixed)	:	Rs. 12-15/kg
Beer Bottles (per bottle)	:	Rs. 2.00

Evidently, the collection of plastics waste is more remunerative *vis-a-vis* other consumer wastes. Wastes generated from cold drinks/ coffee/ ice-cream cups and catering containers, which are mostly made of polystyrene, fetch anything between Rs. 15 and Rs. 25 per kg. Clear packaging film and polypacks are also attractive plastics waste items that fetch as much. India's plastics wastes recycling industry presently handles over 0.75 million tonne of different types and grades of plastics waste, including around 38000 tonnes of in-house plastics scrap, which together at the recycled stage are valued at around Rs. 2500 crores. With the expected consumption of plastics ranging between 4 to 5 million tonnes by the year 2001, and corresponding growth of packaging applications (flexible and rigid) including PET bottles' and containers, the waste generated would vary between 1 and 2 million tonnes every year.

Field visits to recycling/reprocessing units and waste dealers markets, have brought to light the need for upgradation of the working conditions of operations, as also the recycling technology. Also, it is important to pay some attention to the social status of rag-pickers and waste collectors who contribute towards clearance of plastics waste from public places and thus play a key role in the environmental management of plastics waste.

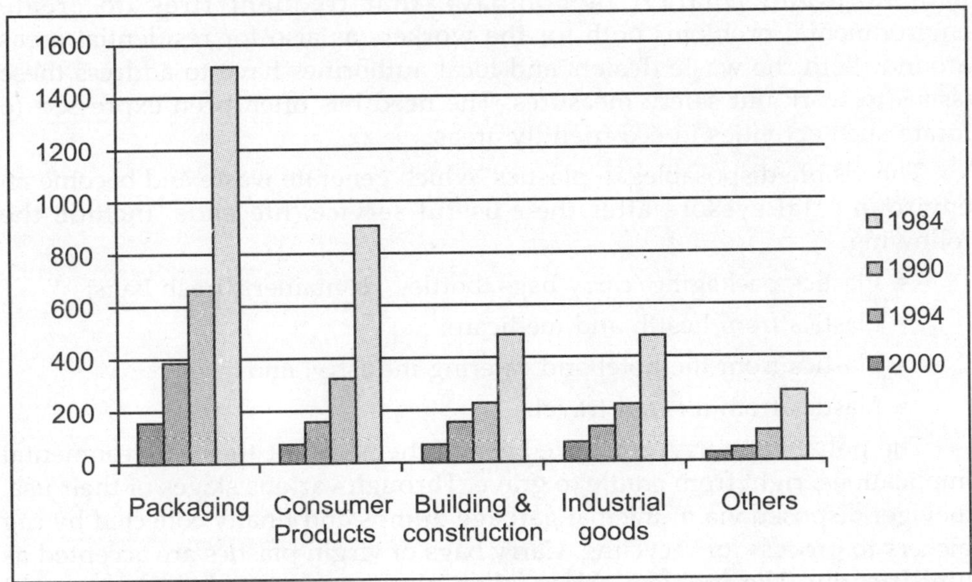

Packaging and Consumer Products Lead the Boom in Plastics Consumption

Packaging is the major application of plastics. Out of 1.88 million tonnes of plastics consumed during 1995-96, over 52 per cent was accounted for packaging applications. This trend is expected to continue. Packaging thus becomes the major source of waste. This includes PE, PVC, Pp, and Multi layer films packaging including around a 30 per cent carry forward of the previous year. This makes .it imperative for the plastics industry to plan its strategy and targets, technologically, socially and environment-ally. This calls for upgradation and diversification of recycling capacity and technology, guidelines' for managing and disciplining plastics waste, maintaining inventory of types, grades and volume of plastics waste generated from various sources, formulating specifications and codes of practices. The need to formulate and issue 'Guideline on Plastics Packaging and Packaging Waste' has been emphasised during various meetings of the Task Force. This has been based on a similar Directive issued by European Union.

To promote increased use of recycled plastics, and upgrading the consumer product applications, there is also a need for undertaking development work which would aim at volume applications, like 'that for the building and construction industry.

ENVIRONMENTAL ISSUES

The waste plastics markets all over India are so packed and crowded with waste spilting over all (examples: Delhi- Asia's largest waste plastics market, handling' and trading over 1000 tonnes of waste daily; Jolly Mohala in Bangalore and Dharavi in Bombay), that frequent fires do create environmental problems both for the workers as also for residential areas around. Both the waste dealers and local authorities have to address these issues to work out safety measures. The need has often been expressed to locate such activities in eco-friendly areas.

The visible disposables in plastics' which generate waste and become an environmental eyesore after their useful service, life ends, include the following:

- Plastics packaging/carry bags/bottles/ containers/trash bags;
- Plastics from health and medicare;
- Plastics from the hotel and catering industry; and
- Plastics from air/rail travel.

The polythene carrybags have been in the news for their environmental implications, right from cradle to grave. Through various stages of their use, they get disposed via municipal garbage dumps and finally collected by rag pickers to process for recycling. Carry bags of virgin plastics are accepted as user-friendly. The problem arises when plastics are recycled for repeated use. Because these are produced from wastes, these is an apparent consumer resistance.

The basic question for polythene carry bags is whether they should at all be manufactured using recycled materials (100%) and, if so, of what grade—first, second, third or the like. With repeated recycling, not only does the carrying strength of polythene bags deteriorate, but the very appearance gets repulsive (and at times unhygienic). For consumer acceptance, the recycled material of first grade should be used and in respect of the second grade, it should be a blend of 50:50 (recycled: virgin). However, third grade recycled material use should be discouraged for the manufacture of carry bags. To sustain the use of plastics through carry bags, certain gradation and acceptable consumer quality must be insisted: and adhered to by the manufacturers. The recycled polythene bags are normally priced in the range of Rs 45 to 50 per kg, whereas for the virgin clear/brightly coloured bags, the price per kg is around Rs. 80. What is worse is that a major volume of more-than-once recycled bags remain on ground, and are not collected by the rag pickers as their resale value gets reduced, these together with other food, vegetable oil and detergents packaging (PP, Polyester, multilaye film) when not collected/recycled, become an eye-sore.

In respect of health and medicare, items in plastics, such as disposable syringes, glucose bottles; blood, and uro bags intravenous tubes and catheters, and surgical gloves, though designed for single use and manufactured with appropriate plastics materials, find themselves under attack, when these are carelessly disposed off Some of these items even return to the market without disinfection. There have been reports of organised picking from garbage dumps around major city hospitals. Such a practice is dangerous and calls for strict action. MoEF has notified rules for management of biomedical wastes which includes plastics wastes.

Plastics items (commonly of PS/PE/PVC/PET) used in the hotel and catering industry, air and rail travel are prominently identified, and after their use, are seen carefully disposed of through 'Dustbins/trash bags' placed in the vicinity. These disposed plastics items are quickly cleared by rag pickers/wastes collectors, and go for recycling at a premium price. Depending upon the scale of operation, a fast-food/catering establishment generates between 5-75 kg of plastics waste/day. Whatever may be the merits of disposables in plastics, once their useful service life is over, they are looked down upon as eyesores in the garbage dumps.

PVC mineral water bottles, and PET liquor and mineral water bottles have invaded the market in India, as a replacement for conventional glass bottles. It is reported that around 7000 tonnes of PVC resin per annum are consumed for the manufacture of mineral water bottles and about 70 per cent gets transferred to the waste stream within four days after one time use. Because PVC is of premium grade, the used bottles are efficiently collected back for materials recycling. However, in respect of PET mineral water and liquor bottles, which are currently marketed in India, around 50 per cent find themselves in waste stream within a week. A 10,000 tonnes capacity exists for manufacturing and marketing of PET mineral water/liquor bottles and assorted containers. Because of durability and glass-like clarity of PET bottles and containers, a major share of these become a long term asset for the users. However, around 50 per cent of current consumption of 6000 tonnes of PET mineral water/liquor bottles used, are available for recycling. Considering the average weight of 27 g per bottle, 3000 tonnes of PET would amount to 115 million numbers of bottles going into waste that largely remains uncollected and unsold. This figure will multiply four-fold by 2001. A system of organised collection of PET bottles waste is required to be encouraged through waste collectors/dealers. Recycling of PET waste is undertaken in Indian by units in Chennai, Gajraula, Kanpur and Mumbai. The existing recycling capacity is required to be fully utilised with generation of PET waste from increased use of mineral water/liquor and soft drink bottles. Appropriate product applications are to be identified and promoted in India.

Depending upon the capacity, a passenger airline per trip generates 5-10 kg of plastics waste. This includes PE/PP film, PS cups, PVC/PET bottles. This waste is identified and graded at source and goes for ready recycling.

REGULATION AND LEGISLATION: PRESENT STATUS

Until recently, there has been no definite environmental policy and legislation framed in respect of plastics waste management in India. The HP Non-biodegradable Garbage (Control) Act, 1995, introduced by the Government of Himachal Pradesh, envisages prohibition of throwing or deposing plastic articles in public places and to facilitate the collection through garbage in identifiable and marked garbage receptacles for non-biodegradables, placed at convenient places, Provisions of this Act, including those of existing laws" for imposing deterrent penalties may be referred to by the local authorities.

The Ministry of Environment and Forests (MoEF) has issued the criteria developed by CPCB in association with the Bureau of Indian Standards for labelling 'plastic products' as 'Environment-friendly' under its 'Ecornark' scheme. One of the requirements for plastic products is that the material used for packaging shall be recyclable or biodegradable. Suggestions for recycled plastic products are quoted.

At present, there are no guidelines or codes of practices for collection, sorting and recycling of plastics waste in the absence of which the conventional practices are adopted and accepted, though need has been voiced to upgrade these, both by the authorities and NGOs. However, while formulating Indian standard specifications for various plastics products, used for critical applications, like plastic piping system, water-storage tanks, packaging for food articles etc., a clause is included which reads "no recycled plastics waste shall be used". An exercise has also been carried out by the Ministry of Environment and Forests in association with the Bureau of Indian Standards to include use of recycled plastics wastes wherever appropriate in the manufacture of plastic products, and this shall be specified accordingly in the relevant Indian Specifications.

The Prevention of Food Adulteration Department of the Government of India, has issued directives of various catering establishments to use only food-grade plastics, while selling or serving food items. Rules have specified use of 'food-grade' plastics, which meet certain essential requirements and are considered safe, when in contact with food. The intention is to preventing possible contamination,' and to avert the danger from use of recycled' plastics. The scheme announced in February, 1995, is being implemented in cooperation with the Bureau of Indian Standards (SIS) which has formulated a series of standards on this subject. The Bureau of Indian Standards Sub-committee PCD 12:17 is charged with formulating guidelines, codes and specifications for recycling of plastics. Two documents *viz.* 'Guidelines for Recycling of Plastics', and 'Recycled Plastics for Manufacturing of Products-Designation' have been finalised by BIS. These two documents, together with the 'Guideline on Plastics Packaging and Packaging Waste' are to be implemented by the industry.

Plastics have become a symbol of our throw-away society. They are non-biodegradable, but recyclable. With the technological advances, plastics recycling is economically feasible for plastics packaging. Recycled materials compete with virgin materials in terms of price and performance. It is an established fact that without reuse, total/absolute diversion of material from waste stream is impossible.

To enhance the demand for recyclable materials, various mechanisms and options are to be assessed. These include: user charge or a tax to ensure that individuals and companies bear the cost of solid waste containing the plastics they produce; government procurement policies, *i.e.* certain percentage of purchased products be recyclable or made of recycled materials, or price preference on items containing recycled material be encouraged, and finally, through recycling standards (meaning thereby that either the products or packaging be made or recyclable material, *i.e.* the material must reach a specified recycling site, or products or packaging consist of a certain percentage of recycled material and this should be appropriately labelled on the product. The advantage of recycling standards, if properly designed and applied is that they provide mechanism for coordinating recycling activities, and for establishing broad-based recycling infrastructure.

As an illustrative and useful example for recycling, the one taken by the Irish Business and Employers' Confederation and the Irish Department of the Environment at Dublin Castle, deserves special mention. Repak is the result of a challenge to industry to develop a scheme funded and organised by the industry to recycle packaging waste. It is an excellent example of a self-regulatory approach to implementation of environmental policy. In the United States, competitive nonregulatory recycling systems are responsible for recycling over 25 per cent of the total municipal wastes, with recycling having doubled over the past decade.

Plastics Waste Management Status in India

	1995-96 Estimates by 2001 (Thousand Tonnes)	
Consumption of Plastics	1889 %	4374 %
Waste available for Recycling	800 %	2000 %
Total	**2689**	**6374**

(% of plastics waste in MSW 1-4% by wt.)

STRATEGY AND ACTION PROGRAMME

As a result of various meetings and discussions with the industry and experts, and the field visits to waste collection and) recycling centres, the Task Force identified the following strategy and action programme.

Target

Evolving integrated plastics waste management policy, with priority for increase in total recovery in terms of materials and energy.

Mission

(*i*) Raising consumer and public awareness, upgrading methodology of waste collection and segregation promoting social and environmental status of waste collectors/rag pickers, who are responsible for collection of plastics waste in India;

(*ii*) Evolving plastics waste management system with appropriate guidelines and directives; and

(*iii*) Promoting upgradation, technically and environmentally, of recycling/ reprocessing systems/technologies, and end products applications with desired recycled content, and formulating guidelines.

Issues of Concern

Communicational

Social and consumer awareness, to promote proper disposal culture through identified and appropriately located dust bins, both in public places, residential, institutional and industrial areas, including hotels and catering establishments, through audio-visual media, publications/ newsletters/video films/posters etc./exhibitions/seminars/workshops.

Technical and Environmental

- Plastics packaging, consumption, waste generation, collection and disposal;

- Evolving plastics waste management system;
- Upgradation of materials recycling technology;
- Social and environmental issues relating to working conditions in plastics recycling industry;
- Limits to materials recycling; and Technology-based incineration to recover energy.

Industrial

To promote Government-industry interaction, and consumer awareness in respect of plastics waste recycling and demand for recycled content in products through:

(*i*) Systematic applications developmental research for promoting end products, their codification/ standardization into critical and non-critical areas:

(*ii*) Industry initiatives and stewardship, by promoting shared producer-user responsibility.

(*iii*) Legislation approach; Incentives/penalties for checking the growth of plastics packaging waste;

(*iv*) Industry-funded and government supported institutional setup with a view to promoting industry's cause towards plastics waste management through setting up of Indian Centre for plastics in the Environment (ICPE).

INTEGRATED APPROACH FOR PLASTICS WASTE MANAGEMENT

The strategy for effective management of plastics wastes should entail the three *R*'s: Reduction, reuse and Recycling of wastes. Hence, the action programme suggested by the Task Force includes a package of Preventive, Promotinal and Mitigative (PPM) measures to achieve these objectives. The implementation of the strategy will require active involvement of all sections of the society in which the industry and the civic authorities are the key partners. They have to act in unison to discharge their responsibilities. Public participation and catalytic support from the government are the two important prerequisites for implementation of the strategy.

The action programme for implementation of the strategy covers the following components:

(*i*) *Preventive measures:* Minimising use of plastics, segregation of wastes and compliance of environmental guidelines;

(*ii*) *Promotional measures:* Improvement in waste collection system and recycling technologies;

(*iii*) *Mitigative measures:* Public awareness programme and penalties for littering, fire protection and safety measures.

Institutional Mechanism

Establishment of a network of concerned Industry Associations, and the Indian Centre for Plastics in the Environment (ICPE), for government-industry interaction.

ACTION PROGRAMME

- **Guidelines on Plastics Packaging:** Packaging constitutes 52 per cent of plastics consumption. Accordingly, this issue was addressed by the Task Force and *Guidelines on Plastics Packaging and Packaging Waste* were prepared. Guidelines lay down measures aimed, as the first priority, at preventing the production of packaging waste, and as additional fundamental principles, at reusing, at recycling, and other forms of recovering packaging waste, and hence, at reducing the final disposal of such waste.
- **BIS Guidelines/Specifications:** The manufacture of products using recycled plastics should follow appropriate BIS *"Guideline for Recycling of Plastics"* and Indian Standard *"Recycled Plastics for the Manufacturing of Products designation"*, which have been finalised by Bureau of Indian Standards (BIS).
- **Limits to Recycling:** Beyond Type-II materials: (Post-consumer plastics waste of unknown origin having visible impurities, as per BIS Guidelines), recycling of plastics waste should be banned. Alternatively, use of such plastics wastes (beyond Type-II) should be resorted to for energy recovery. Recycling of multilayer film packaging and plastics wastes beyond Type-II also be considered for use as composites and volume applications, such as substitutes for wood/ concrete products.
- **Circulation of Dirty Coloured Plastics Carry-bags/Products:** Consumer items, such as toys, water bottles, Kodum, carry bags etc., should not be allowed to use recycled plastics wastes, beyond Type-I (100%). Instead a blend with virgin plastics be encouraged (50:50), and efforts should be made not to downgrade the quality and performance of end products. Reprocessors using dirty plastics wastes for the manufacture of consumer items will be warned of the environmentally unsound practice. Manufacture of dirty coloured carry-bags with visible contamination and their circulation in the market should be banned.
- **Recycling Logistics:** The integrated plastics wastes management need the cooperation and participation of plastics industry, local authorities and the consumers. The industry needs to take the lead in supporting pilot collection schemes with the objective of channelising more and more post-consumer plastics wastes for recycling.

- **Consumer Awareness Programme:** Social and environmental issues relevant to the plastics industry should be addressed by the industry. For this, it is recommended that a country-wide consumer awareness programme be launched from time to time through media, exhibitions, newsletters, publications, videofilms,posters etc., for the education of common man, environmentalists, government departments, trade associations, educational institutions etc.

Applications of Plastics Waste Management

Recycling of PET bottles

Post-consumer PET (number 1) is often sorted into different colour fractions. This sorted post-consumer PET waste is crushed, pressed into bales and offered for sale to recycling companies. PET flakes are used as the raw material for a range of products that would otherwise be made of polyester.

PVC Recycling

PVC or Vinyl Recycling has historically been difficult to perfect on the industrial scale. But within the last decade several viable methods for recycling or upcycling PVC plastic have been developed.

The most-often recycled plastic, HOPE or number 2, is downcycled into plastic lumber, tables, roadside curbs, benches, truck cargo liners, trash receptacles, stationery (*e.g.* rulers) and other durable plastic products and is usually in demand.

The white plastic foam peanuts used as packing material are often accepted by shipping, stores for reuse.

In Israel successful trials have shown that plastic films recovered from mixed municipal waste streams can be recycled into useful household products such as buckets.

Similarly, agricultural plastics such as mulch film, drip tape and silage bags are being diverted from the waste stream and successfully recycled into much larger products for industrial applications such as plastic composite railroad ties. Historically, these agricultureal plastics have primarily been either landfilled or burned on-site in the fields of individual farms.

PLASTIC IDENTIFICATION CODE

Resin Identification Code

Seven groups of plastic polymers, each with specific properties, are used worldwide for packaging applications (*see table below*). Each group of plastic polymer can be identified by its Plastic Identification code (PIC)—usually a number or a letter abbreviation. For instance, Low-Density Polythylene can be identified by the number 4 and/ or the letters 'LDPE'. The PIC appears inside a three-chasing arrow recycling.

Seven Groups of Plastic Polymers used Worldwide for Packaging Application

Plastic Identification code	Type of plastic polymer	Properties	Common packaging Applications
01 PET	Polyethylene Tereph-thalate (PET, PETE)	Clarity, strength, toughness, barrier to gas and moisture	Soft drink, water and salad dressing bottles; peanut butter and jam jars
02 PE-HD	High Density Polye-thylene (HDPE)	Stiffness, strength, toughness, resistance to moisture, permeability to gas	Water pipes, Hula- Hoop (Children's game) rings, Milk, juice and water bottles; the occasional shampoo/ toiletry bottle.
03 PVC	"Polyvinyl Chloride (PVC)	Versatility, clarity, ease of blending, strength, toughness,	Juice bottles, cling films, PVC piping
04 PE-LD	Low Density Poly-thylene (LDPE)	Ease of processing, strength, toughness, flexibility, ease of sealing, barrier to moisture.	Frozen food bags: squeezable bottles, e.g. honey, mustard; cling films; flexible container lids.
05 PP	Polypropylene (PP)	Strength, toughness, resistance to heat, chemicals, grease and oil, versatile, barrier to moisture.	Reusable microwaveable ware; kitchenware; yogurt containers; margarine tubes: microwaveable disposable take-away containers: disposable cups and plates.
06 PS	Polystyrene (PS)	Versatility, clarity, easily formed	Egg cartons; packing peanuts; disposable cups, plates, trays and cutlery; disposable take-away containers;
07 O	Other (often poly-carbonate or ABS)	Dependent on polymers or combination of polymers	Beverage bottles; baby milk bottles; electronic casing.

The symbol is used to indicate whether the plastic can be recycled into new products.

The PIC was introduced by the Society of the Plastics Industry, Inc. which provides a uniform system for the identification of different polymer types and helps recycling companies to separate different plastics for reprocessing. Manufacturers of plastic products are required to use PIC labels in some countries/regions and can voluntarily mark their products with the PIC where there are no requirements. Consumers can identify the plastic types based on the codes usually found at the base or at the side of tie plastic products, including food/chemical packaging and containers. The PIC is usually not present on packaging films, as it is not practical to collect and recycle most of this type of waste.

Toxic Effects of Plastic Waste

The major chemicals used to make plastic resins pose serious risks to public health and safety. Many of the chemicals used in large volumes to produce plastics are highly toxic. Some chemicals, like benzene and vinyl chloride are known to cause cancer in humans; many tend to be gases and liquid hydrocarbons, which readily vapourize and pollute the air. Many are flammable and explosive. Even the plastic resins themselves are flammable and have contributed to numerous chemical accidents. The production of plastic emits substantial amounts of toxic chemicals (*e.g.* ethylene oxide, benzene and xylenes) to air and water. Many of the toxic chemicals released in plastic production can cause cancer and birth defects and damage the nervous system, blood, kidneys and immune systems. These chemicals can also cause serious damage to ecosystems.

Ethylene oxide is used as a sterilant in hospitals. It is also the principle metabolite of ethene, a precursor to polyethylene plastics and other synthetic chemicals. Ethylene oxide can be measured by gas chromatography in air or biological specimens. Ethylene oxide reacts in the body with hamoglobin.

Many food containers for meats, fish, cheeses, yogurt, foam and clear clamshell containers, foam and rigid plates, clear bakery containers, packaging 'peanuts,' foam packaging, audio cassette housings, CD cases, disposable cutlery, and more are made of polystyrene. J. R. Withey in Environmental Health Perspectives 1976 investigated styrene and vinyl chloride monomer as being similar:

> "Styrene monomer readily migrates from food contained in it. It makes no difference whether the food or drink is hot or cold, or contains fat or water. It is not inconceivable that the animal body behaves as a 'sink' for styrene monomer until the lipid portion of the animal body either becomes saturated (although death would probably occur prior to this event) or the tissues are equilibrated at the same concentration as the exposure atmosphere."

PVC is used for many products including: flooring, toys, teethers, clothing, raincoats, shoes, building products like windows, siding and roofing, hospital blood bags, IV bags and other medical devices. One of it's major ingredients is chlorine. When chlorine based chemicals are heated in the presence of hydrocarbons they create dioxin, a known carcinogen and endocrine disrupter. All PVC production releases dioxin. Other sources of dioxin are: production and use of chemicals, such as herbicides and wood preservatives, oil refining, burning coal and oil for energy, all car and truck exhaust, cigarette.

Plasticizers are used in PVC that migrate into a blood recipient via the blood bag, IV bag, IV tubing, children's toys are made with PVC.

Anyone who receives blood, is on kidney dialysis or has tubes either inserted in them or has liquid or air transported to their body is at risk.

About 85 per cent of medical waste is incinerated, accounting for ten per cent of all incineration in the U. S. Approximately five to fifteen per cent of medical waste needs to be incinerated to prevent infectious disease. The remaining waste, while not posing any danger from infectious pathogens is very dangerous when burned. It contains high volumes of chlorinated plastics including PVC (also the toxic substances mercury, arsenic, cadmium and lead.)

WHAT YOU CAN DO ABOUT PLASTIC POLLUTION

Plastic bags and bottles, like all forms of plastic, create significant environmental and economic burdens. They consume growing amounts of energy and other natural resources, degrading the environment in numerous ways. In addition to using up fossile fuels and other resources, plastic products create littre, hurt marine life, and threaten the basis of life on earth. We are producing over 25 million tons of plastics per year in the United States, a trivial fraction of which is getting recycled. Here are some steps that you can take to reverse the tide of toxic, non-biodegradable pollution so that it will not overtake our planet.

Personal Steps	Comments
Take no plastic bags from the grocer's shelf	Put produce in paper, canvas, and other healthy-fiber bags.
Refuse plastic bags at the check-out counter.	If a clerk throws your box of soap into a plastic bag, ask him or her to replace it in one of your bags. Giver the clerk a copy of "Why I Don't Use Plastic Bags." Our experience has been that they appreciate this information.
Don't buy plastic sandwich bags.	Use wax paper bags, cloth napkins, or re-useable sandwhich boxes (e.g., tiffins).
Buy beverages in sustainable containers	Use only glass bottles or cans.
Don't open another plastic water bottle. Take drinking water from the tap.	Bottled water costs over 1000 times more per litre than water from your tap. Buying our most essential nutrient, water, from corporations represents an abdication of community control of the commons. If you have concerns about water safety, investigate a filter system such as Multi-Pure. Better yet, work with your water district to develop stricter standards for water purity.
Buy fresh produce in Mother Nature's wrappers (shell, rind, husk, etc.).	Pre-bagged produce not only use wasteful packaging, but also tends to come from farther away, consuming more of our dwindling oil supplies in transport.

....(Contd.)

Personal Steps	Comments
Give up Tupper Ware and related products.	Tiffins (stainless steel food containers) are a long tradition in India. They store food well, have longer lives than Tupper Ware and its look-alikes (you've probably seen the fading, corroding, and chipping that occurs to these plastic containers), are more hygienic, and have a certain panache.
Make a habit of thinking about what comes with each thing that you buy.	Look for and reward earth-friendly packaging choice. *e.g.* : • Buy greeting cards in paper boxes instead of clear plastic shells • Ask your florist for flowers wrapped in paper, not clear film • Use pens that re-fill instead of land-fill
Make a habit of thinking more in general.	Conscious consumption is not only good for the earth. It's good for you. "Mindfulness," says Thich Nhat Hanh, "is the miracle by which we master and restore ourselves."
Giver away action sheets.	We will give you copies of • "Don't Think of a Plastic Bag!" • "Why I Don't Use Plastic Bags" • Other articles and background sheets • For copies call Green Sangha at (510) 532–6574.
Encourage stores to change their practices.	Share articles such as those listed above. Ask for a meeting with the manager or owner. We'll join you, or help you prepare for a successful conversation.
Organize a presentation on the hidden costs of plastics.	Members of Green Sangha will be happy to make a presentation for your church, school, civic association, or clur, Call us c/o (415) 459-0176.
Study the materials and make a presentation yourself.	Green Sangha is a member of the Campaign Against the Plastics Plague, which provides a slide show and supporting notes at no cost. We offer trainings on how to make presentations in your communities.
Remove plastic from your office or business, and tell your customers why.	Green Sangha will give you sample articles and displays for your restaurant, grocery store, or hotel, explaining to customers the benefits of replacing platic packaging and reducing waste in general.
Get involved hands-on	Help clean up the mess! Across the state, over 290 non-profit and governmental agencies organize volunteer efforts to clean up the coast and prevent pollution. For example, in Marin County:

10 Electronic Waste Management

IT's Underbelly

India produces about 400,000 tonnes of electronic waste each year, growing exponentially. Handling this is a great challenge. What adds to it is the fact that the country is one of the lead importers of all kinds of waste—hazardous included. Almost all of this is recycled or scrapped by the unorganized sector using the most rudimentary methods that pollute. Our reporters found a thriving 'illegal' trade and dangerous working conditions. The environment ministry's answer has been to grant its first and only licence to import e-waste to a company called Attero Recyclin—to encourage its Roorkee plant, which it calls a model. Our reporters found Attero reselling e-waste instead of recycling it. The ministry's regulatory attempts do not recognize the small players who actually recycle e-waste.

Attero, India's recognized recycling facility for e-waste, is about 20 minutes from Roorkee. Its walls and gates are about eight feet high. A signboard warns of CCTV. The security guards have orders to prevent outsiders from carrying inside mobile phones, pen drives or cameras.

I was there on May 3, 2010, with a scrap dealer from Moradabad in Uttar Pradesh. We were to meet D B Chhetri, head of administration and security of the plant, a retired Lieutenant Colonel. Security checks and a short walk later, we entered the office around 3 pm. Our meeting started 15 minutes later.

We said we wanted motherboards. Chhetri said he needed motherboards because 'they are precious'. He offered to sell full computers and peripherals. Our conversation was interrupted by a man who walked in; he wanted to buy a Xerox machine. The deal got sealed quickly for Rs. 4,000.

Chhetri then called an assistant to show us around We were taken to a hall in which new computers were stacked. We wanted black computers; about 50 such were in the adjacent building. We decided we wanted 100.

Back at Chhetri's office, we bargained—unsuccessfully. The standard rate for Pentium III machines was Rs 3,000; P IV machines cost Rs 4,000; and black computers commanded an additional Rs. 500. We would be back in a few days. Chhetri asked us to bring motherbcard samples for him.

Kareem, a scrap dealer from Seelampur, joined us on our second visit four days later. Chhetri told us that as per the environment ministry's new rules on e-waste, Attero could not sell its wares officially to vendors from Moradabad and Seelampur—a fake receipt should do, he said. We would try out a sample first before placing the final order.

As we got talking, Kareem promised Chhetri he would buy truck-loads of waste from Attero. Soon after, Chhetri took us to the godown. It was nothing short of a supermarket. Printers, printer cartridges, computer cabinets, hard disks, floppy drives, fax machines, Xerox machines—they were all there, neatly stacked in columns with their names labelled on signboards. Kareem checked the cost of each product. Keyboards cost Rs 20, SMPS (switched mode power supply, which transmits power from a source to the load, such as a computer) for Rs 55.

I chose a Dell Pentium IV with a 17-inch monitor, which had the serial number 3KKK81S. The Windows XP operating system was functional, I checked.

Chhetri signed the bill, in the name of my scrap dealer friend from Moradabad, on plain paper. As I left the premises, the security guard kept the bill and gave me a photocopy.

I had just bought a computer for Rs 4,500 from a registered recycler that boasts of being India's only end-to-end recycling facility.

After Arnab gave me a heads-up, I was prepared for the security checks. Four officials of Attero—CEO Nitin Gupta, Research and Development Director Praveen Bhargava, Administration and Security Head D B Chhetri and Plant Head Param Prakash—greeted my colleague Sayantan Bera at the building's reception.

Chhetri explained why security was crucial for the Rs. 35-crore plant—they had developed the recycling technology in their laboratories and did not want it leaked. Gupta walked us around the plant's four units—shredder and separator, smelter, electro refinery, and research and development facility.

It can process 36,000 tonnes of waste in a year, though it gets only 600 tonnes at present. Hence it imports e-waste from developed countries. Gupta said formal recyclers like them found the going difficult given the competition from the unorganized sector.

After we got possession of the computer Arnab had bought, I sent Gupta an e-mail. He replied; "As a company policy we do not sell an e-waste to the unorganized sector. We have a very transparent and open culture at Attero, as you might have witnessed during your plant visit." Attero sold refurbished computers only if companies allowed it to refurbish and sell them, and they make their take-back policy clear when they sell it.

Arnab, though, did not get any such directives from Attero.

Sources in the Central Pollution Control Board said e-waste recycling units are not allowed to sell e-waste. They could sell refurbished computers if they have the board's permission for it. Besides, Attero's licence expired in December last year and that makes it illegal to buy, sell or recycle e-waste, the official said.

Naveed, along with his wife Khalida and their three daughters, wakes up every morning to extract gold and copper from circuit boards of dismantled computers (see: *graphic*). He can tell without dirficulty which motherboard is from China, and which one from Japan. The Japanese circuit boards are better, he says, because they fetch him more copper and gold than the ones from China. As he burns the computer parts the plastic melts, emitting a red, toxic fume. The remains from the burnt heap—the metals—fetch him up to Rs 300 per day.

Living in a one-room house in Uttar Pradesh's Moradabad town, Naveed has extracted metals for over 30 years now. Outside his house, in the Nawabpura colony, the locality is full of such one-room houses with dismantled parts of circuit boards strewn all over. Every family here specializes in one of the processes to extract metals from circuit boards. Some use gas torches to heat a board just enough to melt the solder, which separates the metal containing parts from the boards. Some acid-bathe parts, and some, like Naveed, burn the boards.

The circuit boards are sourced from computer monitors, CPUs, keyboards, television and remote control sets, radios, cell phones and other electrical appliances that find their way into the township. Traders estimate about half the circuit boards used in appliances in India end up in Moradabad, also called *peetal nagri*—brass city.

The residents are immune to the smoke, the noise and the smell their work produces. Most of the township's population extract metals on their own, or work with big traders, earning about Rs 100 per day.

Their processes are rudimentary—and risky. Two motherboards, ususally weighing one kg, cost Rs 230. After selling the metals, they get a profit of

10 per cent. They ensure nothing gets wasted. "The poorest people in town even buy the dust that remains after burning the circuit boards to look for traces of copper," said Salim, Naveed's neighbour.

Seelampur: Where e-waste Collects

Salim, 24, entered the recycling e-waste business recently. His brother, among the biggest traders of circuit boards in Nawabpura, sources them from Seelampur, the e-waste hub on the northeastern fringe of Delhi. The Seelampur market is also called trie largest electronics dismantling market in the country, where over 50 per cent of used computers end up for sale and recycling. The workers in Seelampur include teenagers such as Shanu, 15, whose hair shines golden in the sun because of copper extracts in it. He dismantles fans found in the CPUs of computers. "Nobody likes going to schools here because we make more money than a government servant does. On good days we extract 10 kg of copper, at Rs 330 per kg," he said. Separating brass and copper from plastic and rubber using a hammer fetches up to Rs 200 every day.

They are all called dismantlers, for their jobs involve getting computers, breaking them into its basic parts and selling motherboards to traders in Moradabad. The remaining metal and plastics do not reach there. These stay in Seelampur.

Seelampur gets e-waste from across northern India. All scrapped computers that are auctioned in the region wind up in Seelampur. Another source is kabadiwalas (wastepickers) who buy scrapped electronics from households. But almost half the computers are broken pieces from lots of imported secondhand computers.

Auction News, a bi-weekly journal in Delhi, publishes advertisements on scrap that offices or government departments want to auction. When cyclers gather in the offices concerned, auctions are held. In some cases, scrap is sold by inviting tenders.

But, with the government announcing in late April rules on e-waste to regulate the informal e-waste markets, the lives of Naveed, Salim and Shanu, and thousands of others engaged in the industry, might change.

Traders in Seelampur and Moradabad have heard about the announcement but don't know what it means. They apprehend they might be out of business, but are not sure.

Regulating the Informal Sector

More than 90 per cent of the e-waste generated in the country lands up in the unorganized market, a MAIT-GTZ report estimated. MAIT is an association of IT companies, and GTZ works worldwide on sustainable development. City labourers find this work a lucrative opportunity to make money even with the hazards involved, the study said.

The government assumes it will be able to regulate the informal e-waste sector through its proposed rules on e-waste, which allow only registered companies with updated and safe technologies to recycle e-waste. Scrap dealers got to know of the rules at a recent auction by the Reserve Bank of India in Delhi to sell its old computers and printers. The bank rejected a recycler's bid because he did not belong to the organized sector, the recycler said.

"Getting registered means having a large area and and technology. Only those with big investments can get registered," said Daljeet Singh who attended the auction. He runs a recycling store in Mayapuri in Delhi. Most recyclers from the informal sector at the auction have studied till class VIII, said Abdul Rasheed, another scrap dealer from Turkman Gate in Delhi. "Our livelihood depends on these auctions," he said. Rasheed is a regular at such auctions and he sells electronic scrap to traders in Seelampur.

Occupational and Environmental

- **Lead:** A neurotoxin that affects the kidneys and the reproductive system. High quantities can be fatal. It affects mental development in children. Mechanical breaking of CRTs (cathode ray tubes) and removing solder from microchips release lead as powder and fumes.
- **Plastics:** Found in circuit boards, cabinets and cables, they contain carcinogens. BFRs or brominated flame retardants give out carcinogenic brominated dioxins and furans. Dioxins can harm reproductive and immune systems. Burning PVC, a component of plastics, also produces dioxins. BFR can leach into landfills. Even the dust on computer cabinets contains BFR.
- **Chromium:** Used to protect metal housings and plates in a computer from corrosion. Inhaling hexavalent chromium or chromium 6 can damage liver and kidneys and cause bronchial maladies including asthmatic bronchitis and lung cancer.
- **Mercury:** Damages brain and kidneys, impairs foetus growth and harms infants through mother's milk. It is released while breaking and burning of circuit boards and switches. Mercury in waterbodies can form methylated mercury through microbial activity. Methylated mercury is toxic and can enter the human food chain through aquatic iifeforms.
- **Beryllium:** Found in switch boards and printed circuit boards. It is a carcinogen and causes lung diseases.
- **Cadmium:** A carcinogen. Long-term exposure causes Itai-itai, which affects kidneys and softens bones. Cadmium is released into the

environment as powder while crushing and milling of plastics, CRTs and circuit boards. Cadmium may be released with dust, entering surface water and groundwater.

- **Acid:** Sulphuric and hydrochloric acids are used to separate metals from circuit boards. Fumes contain chlorine and sulphur dioxide, which cause respiratory problems. They are corrosive to the eye and skin.

New Rules are Welcome

Organized recyclers, who formed e-waste recyclers' association in July 2009, are cheering the new draft. One of their complaints is they are unable to make profits because of competition from the unorganized market. According to the association, about 10 per cent of the total share of the e-waste market is with organized recyclers.

A 10,000 sq ft formal e-waste dismantling unit in Noida can process up to 500 tonnes of e-waste annually. Since June 2008, when it was launched, the unit has processed only 200 tonnes because of lack of collection mechanisms, said Raj Singh, Noida unit head of TIC Group India Pvt Ltd.

Clients of the formal recyclers include multinational companies that do not want their products to enter the grey market and compete with their new products. "Business process outsourcing companies want their machines processed by formal recyclers to keep up an environment-friendly image. A certificate to this effect is awarded," said Singh. "We cannot match payments of the unorganized sector. Unlike them we scrap all that we get from the companies. Informal dealers refurbish and make money from say a computer, which is a substantial quantum of e-waste," he added. Informal recyclers argued if any part is found in working condition, it is a resource and it makes sense to refurbish it. They usually sell any part of a computer that is functional and it fetches them more money than what they would get if they broke it into metal and sold it.

India generated 330,000 tonnes of e-waste in 2007, which is equivalent of 110 million laptops, said the report by MAIT-GTZ. About 10 per cent of the e-waste generated every year is recycled; the remaining is refurbished. The only way to sustain formal business in the given situation, said the association's members, is the licence to import. Only Attero has the licence to import. Applications from other formal agencies are pending with the environment ministry.

Economics of e-waste Imports

Importing e-waste makes financial sense for the exporter country. For instance, waste traders in Europe or USA, who would have to pay US $20 to recycle a computer safely in their countries, sell it at half the cost to informal traders in developing countries illegally.

In the late 1980s, environmental regulations in industrialized countries and the rise in waste disposal costs led "toxic traders" to ship hazardous waste to developing countries. Basel Convention, an accord signed by 173 countries, mandated that developed nations notify developing nations of incoming hazardous waste. It said that unless the receiving government had legal structure that allowed imports for reasons such as recycling, export of hazardous waste from developed countries to the developing countries was illegal in principle. But the accord did not throw much light on e-waste. Even India's hazardous waste management rules do not factor in e-waste import. This has helped the trade in Seelampur and Moradabad.

Will the environment ministry's proposed e-waste rules manage to organize the informal sector?

Informal *v.* Formal Operators

Dismantling a computer into its basic parts is not hazardous. Then begins the dirty work.

Informal

- Cathode ray lubes' (CRTs) are broken down manually to separate its components—glass, metal and copper. The glass, comprising lead, is sold to bakeries or bangle makers. Since it retains heat, the glass goes into the base of ovens. Phosphors, if inhaled, can be toxic. The CRTs can be sold to non-branded television makers.
- Circuit boards have gold-plated brass pins, microchips and condensers. Heating separates these components. Fumes released during heating are toxic. Gold-plated brass pins are soaked in acid to recover the gold and brass separately. Microchips and condensers are heated in big containers filled with acid to extract metallic parts.
- No safety precautions followed. Informal recyclers paid Rs 200-300 daily in Seelampur; Rs 100-150 in Moradabad.
- Minimal capital investment required. Cost includes price of e-scrap, bribes to tranfer it across state borders and set up and run shops, and rent for the workspace.

Formal

- Components of cathode ray tubes are separated by heating in a closed chamber, which sucks out phosphors from the components. They are then crushed in shredder machines. The glass that contains lead is sold to companies that manufacture CRTs.
- Circuit boards are crushed in shredder machines. They are sent to approved smelters abroad, where after smelting, at 1200°C, the metals in the circuit board collect together. The plastic gets burnt.

Since smelting is carried out in closed chambers at high temperature, it is not hazardous. The metals—lead, copper, nickel, tin, gold, silver, palladium—are then separated by electro-refining.

- Protective equipments—gloves, masks, shoes, caps—are provided to employees. Rs 5,000 per month paid to unskilled workers.
- Investment for a dismantler is about Rs 30 lakh and for a recycling plant, about Rs 25 crore.

Proposed e-waste (Management and Handling) Rules

- Producer's responsibilities include collecting e-waste generated from the end-of-life of their products, ensure such e-waste is channeled to registered refurbishers, dismantlers or recyclers.
- Dealers in electrical products shall collect e-waste by providing the consumer a box, bin or a demarcated area to deposit e-waste.
- Producers need to comply with threshold limits for the use of certain hazardous substances in electronic equipment. Such reduction can be achieved within three years from the date of commencement of the rules. The Ministry of Information and Technology would be responsible for enforcement of reduction in use of hazardous substances, compliance and for granting incentives and certification for green design products.
- Every dismantler and recycler shall have to be registered.
- No import of used electrical and electronic equipment shall be allowed in the country for charity.
- State pollution control boards or committees responsible for grant of authorization, monitoring compliance of authorization and registration conditions will take action against violations of rules. The Central Pollution Control Board shall monitor the compliance of conditions stipulated for granting registration.

Illegally imported e-waste reaches the Seelampur market every second day, said a 35-year-old trader in Delhi's Nehru Place market. He runs a showroom of laptops and stores secondhand computers in the basement. "I know importing waste is illegal. But as long as ships come in, so do profits. My business of about 40,000 tonnes per annum of old computers is a trickle in the import of secondhand electronics market," he said, requesting his identity be protected.

However, as per the estimates of the Directorate General of Foreign Trade, illegal import of e-waste in the country stands at about 50,000 tonnes annually.

Loopholes in laws facilitate illegal import. The country's EXIM (export-import) policy allows import of secondhand computers not more than 10 years old, besides letting in computers as donations. "These provisions in the EXIM policy are unduly utilized by irresponsible developed economies to dump obsolete computers and computer scrap in our country," said Gopal Krishna, convener of environmental non-profit Toxics Watch in Delhi.

Then there is the Customs Tariff Act that says new computers can be imported in India for free, but it does not mention anything on used computers. "Non-existence of classified categories does not imply that their trade is not allowed in India," said the e-waste trader in Nehru Place.

"Both secondhand and new computers are placed under one head in the Indian Customs Tariff Act and therefore traders mix new computers with the old ones when they export," he added. About 5 per cent of the old computers get damaged to the extent that they cannot be refurbished. These are auctioned to e-waste traders in Seelampur, he explained.

If a consignment of secondhand computers is found without a licence, traders manage to get the material by paying a penalty. "It is rare that such goods are confiscated," an e-waste trader said. There is a chance, though, that the goods of repeat offenders are confiscated. But there are ways to avoid that, too—change the company's name for instance.

"We pay a chartered accountant Rs 10,000 every month to register a new name for our company. That way, there is little chance that the computers we import are confiscated," the trader said.

It is also easy to import "donated computers". The Foreign Trade (Development and Regulation) Act of 1992 provides for donation of computers and its peripherals from zones that have been set up'primarily for export at zero customs duty. Such donations can be made to recongnized non-commercial educational institutions, registered charitable hospitals, public libraries, public-funded research and development establishments and government bodies.

In reality, some traders procure old computers in the name of a donation to a school to get tax benefits. "I can get a registration for school under the Society Act of 1968 without actually establishing such a school," said a trader in Delhi. But, if the new rules on e-waste are implemented he cannot do it anymore. The rules do not allow import of electronics under the category of donation.

Not Quite There

The proposed rules, however, do not recognize the magnitude of transboundary movement of e-waste under different categories, said Aashish Chaturvedi, programme manager of GTZ. "It only declares imports for charity illegal. What about the other ways rough which e-waste is imported? For example, under the pretext of metal scrap and secondhand electrical appliances. Electronics can now be imported for refurbishing and repair," he added.

The proposed rules, for the first time in India, bring in the concept of extended producer responsibility, making manufacturers liable for safe disposal of electronic goods. It requires manufacturers to take back the products after their life is exhausted and devise discount schemes for consumers who return the products.

The rules aim to promote green designs that limit the use of hazardous chemicals like lead and mercury in their products. "The essence of the proposed rules lies in the responsibilities assigned to manufacturers," said Lakshmi Raghupathy, former director at the environment ministry. She is now part of the e-waste recyclers' association.

But the rules do not detail the business model for collection of e-waste from consumers, said Vinnie Mehta, executive director of MAIT.

The draft also proposes to centralize e-waste management by describing the roles of dismantlers, refurbishers and recyclers by getting them registered. Chaturvedi, who is working on an EU-funded project to help organize the informal sector, said organizations in the sector should be given preference for getting registererd with the Central Pollution Control Board.

"Existing rules target the informal sector because their ways are risky and they cause pollution, but their role must be recognized. They should be helped in geting organized," he added. Government establishments, though, are unfriendly, said informal associations that are trying to or have got registered.

A company called e-waRDD got itself registered in March this year. It used to be an informal association of recyclers in Karnataka.

"It took us four years of training and fulfilling government mandates to get registered with CPCB," said Asif Pasha of e-waRDD. "The government did not offer us help in securing loans or getting land," added Pasha who applied for the registration after training under GTZ. He raised Rs 16 lakh to get the facility registered. Difficulties in the process will only deter other associations that have also been trained by GTZ to apply for registration, Pasha said. Besides, they are yet to get a recycling contract because "big companies look down on them".

Another such outfit, the Harit Recyclers Union, has registered as a society to begin the process of formalizing. Its member Shashi Pandit said the process would be difficult given the lack of government assistance.

The law currently does not provide for any plan to rehabilitate those involved in informal recycling, said a senior environment ministry official.

Switch Possible?

The Department of Industrial Research, which studied the status and potential for e-waste in India in February 2009, said a symbiotic relationship between the formal and the informal sector was crucial. "The informal sector's role in collection, segregation and dismantling e-waste needs to be nurtured to complement the formal recyclers as supply chain partners. They should take on the higher technology recycling processes," the study said.

Efforts to integrate the two did not yield results, said Nitin Gupta, CEO of Attero. He said he was in talks with formal recyclers to get them to sell their printed circuit boards to Attero, but they have not agreed on a price yet. An association of informal recyclers in Seelampur also rejected Attero's proposal because they could not agree on the price, members told *Down To Earth*.

Getting Waste Through Free Trade Agreements

Developed countries are using free trade agreements (FTAs) to export their waste to the developing world. Japan and the EU are currently negotiating with India and a deal is likely to be signed this year. The commerce ministry has not made public details of 30 such deals India is negotiating. The cause for concern is the part of the draft text of an FTA between the EU and India, which was leaked, and Japan and Thailand, which is in advanced negotiations.

The leaked draft negotiation text of India-EU phrases a new name for waste: it mentions "non-new goods shall be understood to include notably used and re manufactured goods" and that "non-new goods" would not have any restrictions such as import or export tariffs. Thus, import of waste could be treated just like import of fresh products.

Should the deal with India follow the manner in which Japan is trying to seal a deal with Thailand, import of waste in India would "increase enormously which would severely hamper environmental safeguard measures", said lawyer Kajal Bharadwaj.

Since 2004, the governments of Japan and Thailand have been formally negotiating an FTA that seeks to eliminate tariffs on an unprecedented list of Japanese hazardous waste exports to Thailand. According to reports, officials from Thailand's foreign ministry confirmed that the country would have to accept waste, including slag, residues from incinerated municipal waste, chemical and allied industries and hospital waste.

Single Window Dumpyard

India wants global waste. So it gets what it wants

Three months ago, in March, customs officials at the Tuticorin port in Tamil Nadu seized 20 containers carrying 500 tonnes of diapers, sanitary napkins, undergarments, surgical gloves—all used—along with shoe soles, broken toys, perfume bottles, aluminium foil packing material, batteries and bottles. These products, labelled waste paper consignment, were on their way for reprocessing from Greece and Reunion island to a paper factory in Sivakasi town.

The paper manufacturer, Sripathi Paper and Boards, was penalized for illegal import of hazardous waste and asked to export the containers and bear its expenses, said S Chandramohan, additional commissioner of the Tuticorin port. A similar incident happened in 2007-08 at the same port. It turned out that ITC Ltd's mixed waste paper consignment—40 containers—had high concentration of municipal solid waste. The next year the company returned the containers to the US as per a court order.

These are but a few success stories. Customs officials acknowledged their inability to check every container because of shortage of men and machinery. They resort to random checks—in the case of Sripathi Paper and Boards' consignment the department's intelligence team tipped off customs officials. Besides, it gets difficult because the department has to depend on engineers from pollution control board to determine whether a substance is hazardous.

Of the 12 major ports and 14 intermediate ports in India, one—J N port at Nhava Sheva in Mumbai—has two scanning machines. More than a million containers arrive at the port and it is impossible to scan every container, said Yash Vardhan, director of Container Corporation of India. The scanners have limitations. If cobalt-60, a radioactive substance, is packed in a lead box, the scanners would detect the lead because the metal blocks radiation from cobalt-60. "How should the customs department detect it?" asked Vardhan.

Beaches and small ports have grown to be hubs for illegal import of hazardous waste, said a senior customs official asking not to be named. "However much we try, several hazardous waste consignments bypass us," he added.

Matchmaking, Online

The standard procedure followed for importing a consignment to India involves an importer, an exporter, an agency registered and notified by the Directorate General of Foreign Trade, a bank and the customs department at the port. First, the importer is required to get a pre-inspection certificate of the import material by a registered agency, which could be an Indian or a foreign company.

After the agency issues the certificate, a bill detailing the number of containers, excise duty classification and product details is prepared. Then the consignment is shipped. When it reaches India, customs officials at the port check the certificate, levy a customs duty on the product as specified in the Central Excise Tariff Act and release the consignment to the importer.

If the material imported turns out hazardous, like in the Shivakasi 'wastepaper' import, it is returned to the exporter, without a customs duty. Or not returned at all. "Confiscation of goods on such imports is rare. Imposition of a fine is part of organized corruption at the ports where customs clearance agents bribe customs officials," a customs clearance agent in Kandla said. An official of the Directorate General of Foreign Trade also acknowledged that at times customs officials allow importers to escape the full penalty by an underassessment of illegally imported goods.

Then there are times the importers are genuinely cheated. That is because they look for information on registered agencies and exporters mostly on the Internet. This has its share of risks—the biggest is that of getting cheated, importers say. Exporters show photographs of a consignment, pure iron scrap for instance, but it turns out different—mixed scrap—when it reaches the importer. Inspection can be done by checking the total amount of goods and verifying compliance with the standards of the destination country.

Table 10.1 Hazardous Waste Imports of India

Substance	2007-08 (Qty in tonnes)	2008-09 (Qty in tonnes)
Ash and residue from incineration of municipal waste	5,192.72	39,713.29
Other Waste Organic Solvents	2.14	2.00
Waste paring & Scrap of Pet bottles and plastic*	144,434.00	441,299.54
Lead waste and scrap*	16,470.00	25,843.77
Waste of iron and steel scrap*	3,340,057.483	4,261,091.067
Other waste oil	139,530.00	35,670.00
Waste Imports in India (total)	**3,645,686.343**	**4,803,619.667**

*List of hazardous wastes applicable for import and export not requiring prior informed consent.

Source: Website of Department of Commerce.

In India, the Union Ministry of Environment and Forests decides on what hazardous waste can be imported and exported. Under the Hazardous Waste (Management, Handling and Transboundary Movement) Rules, the ministry has placed import of hazardous waste items under three categories—substances that can be imported with prior consent, free imports under Open General Licence and prohibited.

The first category includes metal and metal-bearing wastes of antimony, lead, galvanic sludges and waste lead acid batteries, whole or crushed. An importer is required to have a licence from the Directorate General of Foreign Trade. The list in the second category comprises materials such as iron, steel and zinc scrap; lead scrap except lead acid batteries; waste of copper and its alloys. The waste listed in this category are traded under Open General

Licence. The third category, prohibits import of waste contaning mercury, beryllium, arsenic, selenium and thallium.

Over 10,000 items, hazardous included, are imported in India, commerce ministry officials said. These items are classified under various heads. The category 'others' is given to those items that cannot be classified under any head. Even the environment ministry does not know how to describe categories such as 'other waste and scrap'. Traders often end up making use of 'others'.

Secondary Markets

Different types of metal scraps are available in the international market. If I wish to import steel scrap and am not sure whether it's pure, I would put it in the category of'other waste and scrap.

Steel scrap is used to prepare secondary steel, of which India has one of the biggest markets in Asia. "With the scrap, input cost for preparing secondary steel reduces by 10 per cent. This helps earn more profits," said a secondary steel manufacturer in Punjab who did not want to be named.

India's secondary steel market has come under the scanner because of manufacturing defects—several times the steel made from scrap was found to be radioactive. In 2009 German magazine *Spiegel Online* reported that radioactive steel imported from India was on the rise in Germany. The country seized 150 tonnes of contaminated metal exported by India between August 2008 and February 2009. In October 2008, radioactive substances were found in 500 elevator buttons prepared by French company Otis.

France imported the raw material used in the buttons from India. Five scrap recycle companies were held responsible.

But Why Import?

Recyclers in India say since they don't get enough waste in the country, they are forced to import such waste.

India produces 6.2 million tonnes of hazardous waste annually, according to Central Pollution Control Board's 2008 data. According to the board, hazardous waste generation is high in Gujarat, Maharashtra, Andhra Pradesh, Chhattisgarh and Rajasthan. These states do have common hazardous waste treatment, storage and disposal facilities, but not all the waste reaches the facilities.

There are pilferages, but it's the duty of state pollution control boards to plug these loopholes, said an official of the environment ministry. A lot of the waste, added an environmental engineer from the Central Pollution Control Board, is disposed of into rivers, drains or landfills.

India imports most of its metal scrap from the US, the UK and the Arab countries. As per the US Institute of Scrap Recycling Industries, the country's exporters in 2005 shipped more than US $350 million of scrap commodities to India.

In 2003-05, the Centre allowed import of 3.4 tonnes of cobalt waste and scrap, 101.1 tonnes of clinical waste in 2004-05, and 700 kg of sewage sludge the next year. In 2007-08, 0.3 million tonnes of asbestos and its compounds were imported, along with 120.06 tonnes of mercury and its compounds and 428.54 tonnes of arsenic and its compounds.

The choice India faces is this: either it stops importing waste and thereby gives up the option to make money from recycling. Or it imports waste but regulates it better so as to distinguish a resource from what the world wants to dump here unscrupulously.

Chemical Waste Disposal

HAZARDOUS WASTE DISPOSAL PROCEDURES

EHS coordinates disposal of chemical waste from University operations. The cost of waste disposal is borne by EHS, rather than the individual department or laboratory, in part to eliminate any hesitation to properly manage chemical wastes.

The following procedures apply to any chemical substances generated from University operations (including laboratories, administrative units, and physical plant operations) that are classified as hazardous based on the criteria described below. This procedure does not apply to disposal of radioactive or biohazardous wastes.

In order to responsibly manage chemical waste each employee must be familiar with the following:

Hazardous Waste Characteristics

Properly Packaging Waste Materials

Effective labelling

Waste Collection Protocol

Classification of Waste as Hazardous

Waste is considered hazardous if:

- it is on either of two lists of specific chemical substances developed by the Federal Environmental Protection Agency (EPA). Most commonly used organic solvents (*e.g.* acetone, methanol, toluene, xylene, methylene chloride etc.) are included (*see list*). For further information contact Environmental Health and Safety.

- it is on a list of non-specific sources that includes a broad range of spent halogenated and non-halogenated solvents (*see list*).
- it is on a list of specific sources that includes primarily industrial processes.
- it exhibits any of the following characteristics as defined by the EPA (definitions are abbreviated):

❑ **Ignitable**

- a liquid with a flash point less than 60°C
- not a liquid and capable under normal conditions of causing fire through friction, absorption of moisture or spontaneous chemical changes
- an ignitable compressed gas
- an oxidizer

❑ **Corrosive**

- it is aqueous and has a pH less than or equal to 2 or greater than or equal to 12.5
- It is a liquid and corrodes steel at a rate greater than 0.250 inches per year a 55 degrees Centigrade

❑ **Reactive**

- it is normally unstable
- it reacts violently with water
- it forms potentially explosive mixtures with water
- it generates toxic gases, vapours or fumes when mixed with water
- cyanide or sulfide wastes that generate toxic gases, vapours or fumes at pH conditions between 2 and 12.5
- it is capable of detonation or explosive decomposition if subjected to strong initiation or under standard temperature and pressure
- it is classified as a Department of Transportation explosive

❑ **Toxicity Characteristic**

- if an extract of the waste is found to contain certain metals, pesticides or selected organics above specified levels (*see list*).
- if it is otherwise capable of causing environmental or health damage if improperly disposed (this is a judgment you must make based upon your knowledge of the material from the Material Safety Data Sheet or the literature).

Packaging Chemical Wastes

Place hazardous waste in sealable containers. Waste disposal cost is based on volume, not weight therefore, whenever possible, containers should be filled, leaving headspace for expansion of the contents. Often the original container is perfectly acceptable.

If you routinely generate significant quantities of compatible solvents or other liquids, bulking of waste in five gallon carboys provided by EHS may be practical. Savings to the University from this practice are substantial. If you are interested, please call EHS at x8-5294.

The container should not react with the waste being stored (*e.g.* no hydrofluoric acid in glass). Similar wastes may be mixed if they are compatible (*e.g.* non-halogenated solvents).

Whenever possible, *wastes from incompatible hazard classes should not be mixed* (*e.g.* organic solvents with oxidizers). Certain metals also cause disposal problems when mixed with flammable solvents with oxidizers). Certain metals also cause disposal problems when mixed with flammabk (liquids or other organic liquids.

Containers must be **kept closed** except during actual transfers. **Do not leave a hazardous waste container with a funnel in it.**

Chemical containers that have been triple-rinsed and air-dried in a ventilated area can be placed in the trash or recycled. If the original contents were highly toxic, the container should be rinsed firs with an appropriate solvent and the washings disposed of as hazardous waste.

Labelling of Chemical Waste Containers

Containers containing hazardous waste must be labelled with the words HAZARDOUS WASTE along with the names of the principal chemical constituents and the approximate percentage.

Waste container labels can be obtained by contacting Environmental Health and Safety at ×8-5294. Use of these labels is preferred but not mandatory unless the waste will be placed in storage before disposal. If you choose not to use the standard labels, the container still must be labelled with the words **Hazardous Waste**.

Do not list reactants, only products. For example, if a cyanide was used in a reaction but all of the material was oxidized to a cyanate before disposal, do not list cyanide on the label.

Use IUPAC or full chemical names (in English), no abbreviations, symbols, structural diagrams product trade names.

Hazardous Waste

Federal and New Jersey Laws Prohibit Improper Disposal

Department ______________________ Phone________________

Lab Group ____

Responsible Individual_____________________________________

Date Placed in 90 Day Storage______________________________

	Contents	Approximate %
	____________________	____________________
	____________________	____________________
Use IUPAC	____________________	____________________
Nomenclautre	____________________	____________________

Hazard Class (if known)

1. Poison	4. Oxidizer	7. Sensitive to stock,
2.Flammable Liquid	5. Corrosive	Friction, Air or Water
3. Flammable solid	6. Peroxide Former	
896		

Labelling should be accurate and legible and should include the name of the generator, the name of the lab group or PI, the department, and an extension where someone who is knowledgeable about that specific waste can be reached on the day of the pickup in case questions arise during packaging for disposal.

Do not place the date on the label until the day the container is placed in the main collection room. **Date the container with the current date once it is removed from the lab for the waste pickup.**

Disposal Procedure

Chemical Waste Pickups are generally scheduled for the last Thursday of each month, January through October. There is no pickup in November, the following pickup is the second or third Thursday in December. The current schedule follows:

- December 15, 2011
- January 26, 2012
- February 23, 2012
- March 29, 2012
- April 26, 2012
- May 31, 2012
- June 28, 2012
- July 26, 2012

- August 30, 2012
- September 27, 2012
- October 25, 2012
- December 13, 2012

The *Waste Paper* newsletter serves as a notice for each pickup and is distributed to Department I Safety Managers, Chemical Hygiene Officers and other interested persons approximately one week in advance. If you would like to be added to the distribution.

Pickups take place at six main campus locations:

- Lewis Thomas Laboratory loading dock
  - for wastes from Molecular Biology and Genomics departments.
  - The dropoff of waste generated in GeoSciences and EEB labs is handled for GeoSciences. Researchers must contact them for arrangements.
- Jadwin Hall/Frick Chemistry
- Cogen Plant - cogen and chilled water plant waste only
- MacMillan Building - maintenance wastes only
- Engineering School
  - for E-Quad and Bowen
- 20 Washington Road loading dock

Specific arrangements for getting material to the pickup site are the responsibility of the individual departments. Refer questions of this nature to your Department Safety Manager or Chemical Hygiene Officer. Generally, wastes must be at the pickup site by 9 A.M. the day of the pickup to be included.

Eihidium bromide usually does not need to be disposed as hazardous waste. Electrophoresis gels containing trace amounts of ethidium bromide (less than 0.1%) may be placed in regular laborator trash. Gels containing more than 0.1% (usually dark pink or red color) should be placed in the medical waste boxes. Ethidium bromide solutions may be neutralized and disposed down the drain.

Used oil is not disposed as part of the hazardous waste programme, with the following exceptions:

- vacuum pump oil
- cutting oils
- PCB contaminated oil
- oil mixed with hazardous waste

Do not label used oil as hazardous waste. Instead, label the container with the words 'Used Oil', no 'waste oil', along with the names of any other constituents.

Silica gel, molecular sieves and desiccants are not considered hazardous waste unless they are in grossly contaminated. Contaminated silica gel can be recycled.

Uranium and thorium compounds, such as uranyl acetate, uranyl nitrate, uranyl formate, uranium oxide, thorium nitrate and thorium oxide, are considered radioactive waste, rather than chemical I waste.

Chemical wastes that are combined with radioisotopes are considered **mixed waste**.

Do not bring wastes to the pickup site that are not properly identified. It is the chemical user's responsibility to identify and properly label all chemical wastes. The disposal company cannot (legally transport or dispose of unidentified/unknown waste. If they are abandoned at the pickup site they remain the responsibility of the department.

Arrangements for chemical analysis of unknowns can be made through EHS. Costs associated with improper management of hazardous waste (*e.g.* characterization of unknowns, special handling of peroxide forming compounds etc.) are charged back to the generator department.

Storage of Chemical Waste

Containers of hazardous waste may be stored in an area of a laboratory or facilities operation near the point of generation. This area must be controlled by the principal investigator or workers generating the waste. State and federal regulations stipulate how waste generators store chemical waste and require the following:

- Any container used to store hazardous waste must be labeled with the words "hazardous waste" (regardless of its location) as soon as accumulation begins.
- Be sure that the container is *compatible* with the chemical waste.

  Use containers that are made of or lined with materials which will not react with, and are otherwise compatible with, the hazardous waste to be stored. For example, do not place hydrofluoric acid in glass. Often the original container is suitable.
- Waste containers must be closed at all times, except when being filled. Do not leave funnel in the containers.
- Be sure that containers in the waste storage area do not leak. Consider the use of *secondary containment*, such as a tray, larger container or basin. If a leaking container is found, immediately clean up any spilled material according to established spill cleanup procedures and transfer the waste into a container that is in good condition.

- No more than one quart of an acutely hazardous waste (*P-listed wastes*) or 55 gallons of other hazardous wastes may be stored (per waste stream) in the waste storage area. If this threshold quantity is reached, the worker must transfer the waste to a 90-day *storage area* or send it out to an off-site authorized commercial facility within three days. The container must bear a hazardous waste label with the accumulation date (either the date the threshold quantity was reached or the date it was placed in the 90-day storage area) marked on the container.
- Like any chemical storage in the laboratory or work area, be sure to segregate the container according to the type of waste.
- Waste stored near drains (floor, sink, cup sink) should have *secondary containment*. If you have a sink or drain that is not in use, contact maintenance to explore possibilities for plugging or sealing the drain. Secondary containers must be compatible with the waste. Contact EHS for more information.

Waste Compatibility

Chemical waste that are incompatible should not be mixed or stored together. If these wastes must be stored in the same area, they should be physically separated using secondary containment or another means that will prevent the materials from contacting each other in the event of a spill or leak.

The following are sources of information about compatibility:

- BRA Chemical Compatibility Chart
- RCRA Waste Compatibility Chart
- Laboratory Safety Manual Chemical Storage Information
- Mallincrodt Chemical Storage Chart.

Container Compatibility

The container used for hazardous waste collection must be compatible with the waste and must not contain residues of incompatible materials.

The following table shows general chemical categories and compatible container types:

Chemical Category	Container Type
Mineral Acids	Plastic
Bases	Plastic
Oxidizers	Glass
Organics, including acetic acid	Glass

Take special care in choosing containers for the following wastes:

- **Nitric Acid:** reacts with organics (including acetic acid) to produce heat and gas. If product containers for organics are used to collect nitric acid, be sure to rinse thoroughly to avoid potential over-pressurization and subsequent burst of the container.
- **Perchloric Acid and Organic Peroxides:** highly reactive with organics and organic material, such as wood. May also react with metals.
- **Hydrofluoric Acid:** Dissolves glass containers.

Battery Recycling Programme

Alkaline batteries are not rechargeable and do not contain any hazardous materials. From a life cyclic and energy analysis, recycling an alkaline battery is more environmentally detrimental than dispose of it directly in the trash. Princeton University follows this guideline and does not recycle alkaline batteries. Please help our building services staff and discard of these items directly in the trash.

Used batteries containing hazardous metals (*e.g.* mercury, cadmium, lead, and silver) are classifie universal waste rather than hazardous waste. This allows Princeton to recycle the batteries, while continuing to ensure that the batteries are handled in an environmentally sound manner. *Lead-acit batteries* are also recycled.

Building Services administers a collection programme to encourage this recycling effort. Receptacles for Nickel-Cadmium, Nickel-Metal Hydride, Lithium, Lithium-ion, Mercury and Silver batteries have been placed in the stockrooms at Frick, Engineering Quad, Lewis Thomas Lab and Physics. Containers for additional areas are available through Al King at 8-1778. Batteries also may be brought to the Building Services Administrative Offices at 180 Alexander St.

Packaging for Disposal

To guard against possible short circuiting, the Rechargeable Battery Recycling Corporation (established by battery manufacturers) recommends you do at least one of the following to prepare batteries for recycling:

- **Discharge Cells:** This should be done only by a knowledgeable engineer or technician. Consult your battery supplier for instructions on how to discharge cells completely and properly.
- **Terminal Protection:** If you cannot assure that the cells have been completely discharge then cover the terminals of each battery with non-conductive tape.

- **Place in a Plastic Bag:** Batteries may be placed separately in plastic bags so the terminal not come in contact with other batteries or metal during storage or transport.
- Package batteries so that terminals will not short-circuit during storage or transport.

It is important to note that this program is intended only for batteries generated from University operations. Individuals should continue to use curbside recycling, household hazard waste days, and purchase/exchange programmes for the disposal of personal batteries.

Lead Acid Batteries

Lead-acid batteries are collected separately by the University and sent to a recycler.

Biological and Medical Waste Disposal

- Bio-hazardous Waste (Regulated Medical Waste)
- Animal Bedding Waste
- Animal Carcasses
- Patient Care Wastes

Bio-hazardous Waste (Regulated Medical Waste)

Some wastes associated with biological materials must be disposed of in special ways because they may have been contaminated with infectious organisms or agents. These potentially infectious or bio-hazardous materials are defined by NJ regulations as Regulated Medical Waste. These wastes include the following:

- All sharps, *e.g.* glass implements, needles, syringes, blades, etc. coming from facilities using infectious materials
- Biologically-cultured stocks and plates, human blood or tissues

For disposal of these wastes, the lab personnel:

1. Sterilize or disinfect waste materials associated with viral, bacterial or other agents infectious to humans (by autoclave or chemical treatment equivalent to 1:10 bleach solution).
2. Place all bio-hazardous wastes, except for sharps, directly into the red bag-lined medical waste boxes provided by Building Services.
3. Place sharps into labeled sharps containers which when filled are placed into the medical waste box.
4. When the Medical Waste box is filled, seal the bag liner and box and notify janitor for pick-up.
5. Where pick-ups are infrequent or limited, contact Building Services to arrange for pick-up.

Important Labelling Requirement

Lab personnel must apply an adhesive-backed label completed with generator information to each bag or container (such as autoclaved bags or filled sharps containers) placed into the medical waste box. Building Services provides such a label that has space to record Date, Building, Lab #, and Contact Person. Apply this label to all containers placed inside the medical waste box AND to the exterior of the sealed medical waste box before it is made available for pick-up by Building Services. Alternatively, the inner bags and containers can be marked clearly with a permanent marker.

Other wastes generated in these facilities that are not contaminated with biological agents or materials are not treated as biohazardous and may be discarded in the regular trash container, with recyclables, or into other specially designated waste containers. These include such items as recyclable and non-recyclable waste glass, gloves, unused plates or tubes, fly media or embryo plates, etc.

In order to clarify how these various wastes are to be handled in laboratories using biological materials, the *waste stream chart* has been developed and put into use for all departments generating research waste. It is intended for laboratories using biological and/or chemical materials.

Animal Bedding Waste

Animal bedding waste that has been exposed to biosafety level 2 agents is autoclaved prior to disposal or, if an autoclave is not available in the animal facility, is packaged as infectious waste in cardboard fiber drums or boxes by Laboratory Animal Resources (LAR) staff.

Any container of bedding that is labeled as infectious waste is closed by LAR staff to prevent spills or leakage. Containers of infectious waste are picked up by Building Services and transported to a weather-protected shelter for holding until they are picked up by the University's infectious waste vendor, for incineration. Spills from containers of animal bedding labeled as infectious waste are to be cleaned up by LAR staff.

Animal bedding that has *not* been labelled as infectious is bagged and collected for disposal by LAR staff. After bagging the waste, it is placed into gray carts for movement by LAR staff to the pick-up location. This waste is picked up by Princeton University Building Services personnel and is not to be mixed with other waste. Bags are filled only to a depth and weight that will allow for effective tying of the bag by animal facility staff and for ease of handling by one person. For example, several partially-filled bags should be tied and placed in the gray carts rather than one or two full bags (bag weight should not exceed 40 pounds). This will help to prevent repetitive motion injury to staff and prevent bags from being ripped open while being handled.

The carts are maintained clean and in sanitary condition by the animal facility staff. Any spills of (non-infectious) bedding when loading the truck are cleaned up by the Building Services trash crew.

Animal Carcasses

Freezers are provided in each animal facility for storage of carcasses that have been bagged and sealed. All animal carcasses that have been exposed to biosafety level 2 agents are placed into an infectious waste bag. All carcasses are packed and incinerated as infectious waste through a licensed, contracted firm.

Freezers are cleaned and defrosted as necessary by animal laboratory personnel to keep them in a sanitary croom 41 and removed by animal care staff to medical waste boxes for pick-up by Building Services as part of the medical waste stream.

Patient Care Waste Disposal

All disposable wastes generated in hospitals from patient rooms and as part of direct patient care are considered potentially infectious and are disposed of in the medical waste stream. Syringes, needles, and other sharps are placed in the provided sharps container which, when filled and sealed are placed in the provided medical waste box. When boxes are filled and sealed, they are removed by the custodial staff outside to the locked storage shed for later pick-up by Building Services.

Patient care waste generated at other sites on campus by medical response personnel (i.e. Public Safety) are placed in biohazard bags and brought to hospital for medical waste disposal or handled by responding EMS personnel.

A programme is in place to ensure that needles and syringes generated as part of personal diabetes care will not be an exposure hazard to others. Collection containers are available from hospital which, when filled, are returned to Health Centre for proper disposal in the medical waste stream.

Pre-steps to be Taken by Local Bodies and NGO(s)

Measures to Be Taken to Reduce Solid Wastes

The solid waste collected from the door steps or from the community bins through the primary collection system needs to be unloaded and stored at convenient places for its onward transportation in a cost effective manner. Temporary waste storage depots which synchronize with primary collection and transportation system are, therefore, required to be created at suitable locations in lieu of open waste storage site, and in replacement of cylindrical cement bins masonry bins, Dhalavs, etc.

Steps to be taken by the Local Body

The local body, taking into consideration that:

1. There is adequate space to place one or more containers of 3 to 10cu mtr. size;
2. The proposed waste storage depot would not abstract the entrance of any building, would not cause hindrance to the traffic, there is adequate space for the moment of the vehicle which may come to pick up the container should identify suitable locations at a distance not exceeding 250 metres from the work place of sanitation workers where waste storage depots facilities can be created. As far as practicable such depots should be created at the existing unhygienic waste storage depot sites to minimize the objections from the people. As soon as such sites are identified the site should be prepared in such a way that a large size closed body container/containers can be placed at the site and it becomes possible to bring waste up to

such containers easily and transfer the contents from the handcarts. It should also be possible to remove the container or replace with the hydraulic vehicle without causing inconvenience to the people and obstruction to the traffic. Soon thereafter all open waste storage sites should be abolished expeditiously and all dust bins made of cement pipex metal rings, masonry construction, *dhalavs* etc. should also be replaced in a shased manner by a neat mobile container placed at the site identified for depostion of waste through containerized handcarts/containerized tricycles etc, brining waste from the door steps from the community bins and from the streets.

Maintenance of Waste Storage Depots/Containers

A periodical inspection should be carried out once in three months of the waste storage depots and any damage caused to the floorings screen walls etc. should be repaired.

The waste storage containers and handcarts which bring waste to the waste storage depots should be repaired expeditious by as soon as reported by the sweeper and the sweeper should be given replacement against taking this handcart/container foi repair so that his work is not hampered.

The large container generally how a strong frame end the metal sheets of the container get corroded if not well maintained. Annual painting of the container from inside and outside must be carried out for increasing the life and better appearance of the container.

When the metal sheets of the large container give way the entire container need not be replaced only the sheet may be repaired or replaced. It is only when it is felt that its main frame has given way and repairing is not possible the entire container may be replaced. A large container should normally last for 2 to 8 years.

The handcart generally last for 40 to 50 years but its containers may last only for 1 to 2 years. The containers as and when warn out should be replaced maintaining adequate staff of the same in the work-shop or in the solid waste management departmental stores.

Collection

Measures Necessary to Improve the Service

The local body should provide a daily waste collection service to all households, shops and establishments for the collection of putrescibie organic waste from the doorstep because of the hot climatic conditions in the country. This service must be regular and reliable, recyclable material can be collected at longer regular intervals as may be convenient to the waste producer and the waste collector, as this waste does not normally delay and need not be collected daily. Domestic hazardous waste is produced occasionally such waste need not be collected from the doorstep, people could be advised or directed to put such waste in special bins kept in the city for disposal of such waste.

Steps to be Taken

- The urban local bodies may arrange for the collection of domestic, trade and institutional food/biodegradable waste from the doorstep from the community bin on a daily basis.
- The local body may also arrange through NGO's collection of recyclable waste material/non biodegradable waste other than toxic and hazardous waste from the source of waste generation at the frequency and in the manner, notified, by the local body from time to time in consultation uith the NGOs/Resident Association etc.
- Domestic hazardous/toxic waste material deposited by the waste producers in special bin/provided by the local body at various places in the city may be collected at regular intervals after ascertaining the quantities of such uaste deposited in special bins.

TRANSPORTATION

Measures to be Taken to Improve the System

Looking to the present situation, the transportation of waste has to be planned scientifically to bring about a total change in the existing system.

The system of transportation should be such that it can be easily maintained in the city departmentally or through private garages and the system should appropriately match with the system adopted for the storage of waste at the waste storage depots. Manual loading should be discouraged and phased out expeditiously and replaced by direct lifting of containers through hydraulic system or non-hydraulic devices or direct loading of waste into transport vehicles.

Transportation of waste should be done regularly to ensure that the containers/trolleys and dustbin sites are cleared before they start overflowing. The frequency of transportation should be arranged accordingly. The system of transportation of waste must synchronize with bulk storage waste at the temporary waste storage depots multiple and manual handling of waste should be avoided.

Setting Up of Transfer Station

In large cities where the disposal site is more than 10-km away from the city boundary and smaller vehicles are used for the transportation of waste, it may prove economical to set up transfer stations to save transportation time and fuel provided the city has a good performance record of vehicles and containers. Large size 15 to 20 cum containers could be kept at the transfer station to receive waste from small vehicles. A ramp facility may by provided to facilitate unloading of the vehicles or DP containers, directly into large containers at the transfer station, construction of complicated and expensive transfer stations must be avoided. The requirement of large containers and vehicles may be worked out on the basis of the total quantity of waste expected to be bought to the transfer station and the number of trips the vehicles will be able to maxe in two shifts each day.

Lifting of Waste from the Transfer Station

In the cities where transfer stations have been provided, to economize the cost of transportation of waste, the large containers of 15 to 20 cum may be used and lifted by specially designed vehicles which can carry the big size containers duly cleared by regional transport authorities.

Workshop Facility for Vehicle Maintenance

All local bodies must have adequate workshop facilities for the maintenance of their fleet of vehicles and containers handcarts etc. such facilities may be created by the local body departmentally or through a contractual arrangement. The workshop, public or private, should have adequate technical staff spares and preventive maintenance schedules to ensure that at least 80 per cent of the vehicles remain on the road each day and the down time of repair maintenance is minimized to the extent possible. Spare assemblies should be kept available which could be given as replacements until necessary repairs are carried out. The workshop should be preferably headed by an automobile or mechanical engineer.

The cities which use hydraulic equipments such as dumper placers, refuse collectors etc. should as far as possible give away contract to the manufacturer of the equipments or to their, authorized agents or to a reliable workshop in the city for the repairs and maintenance of the vehicles to keep the fleet of vehicles a good condition. In such cases daily checking 15 days checking, checking after 2000 kms and 4000 km may be carried departmental!y and checking after 2000 kms could be got done through a private carriage which has been given a contract. Generally this will take about a one year when some major repairs would require in the vehicles, which could be done through the contractor.

OTHER MEASURES

Community Participation

Community is in the centre of all the activities yet it is ignored by the decision makers and made to merely wait and watch and ultimately what people get in hand is what they do not want or what is not in their priority. This creates a void between the administrators and those administered and an atmosphere of apathy is created which distances people from government initiatives.

Public awareness, effective community participation, transparent and lean administration, introduction of citizen charters and accountability at all levels can only bridge this gap.

SWM is one such activity where public participation is very to success. The local body can never be successful in SWM without active community participation whatever may be the investments made from the Municipal Government funds. The local bodies are the institutions of grass root democracy having elected members from a small group of electorate. It also has an outreach service at the ward level through which it can easily interact with the people on almost all important issues. The local body should therefore seriously consider involving community in all programs through a consultative process and variety of other communication approaches.

Public Information, Education, Communication Programmes (IEC)

For the successful implementation of any programme involving public at large in SWM system, it- is essential to spell out clearly and make them known to the people the manner in which local body proposes to tackle the problem of waste management and extent to which public participation in SWM is expected to keep the city clean and improve the quality of life in the city.

- Ensure that the people become aware of the problems of waste accumulation and the way it affects their lives directly.
- Ensure that the people generate less waste by cutting back on waste generating material and by following clear defined practices of waste management.
- Create public awareness against big waste generators and provide information to monitor the performance of these sources of waste.
- Inform the people about waste management programme of the Government and municipal bodies.
- Promote public participation in waste management efforts through private partnership where feasible.
- Propagate the message that the "Clean City Programme" is both analytical and purposive and that solution proposed all within the frame work of Govt. initiatives and legally appropriate.

Citizens co-operation is vital to reduce, reuse and recycling of waste and in keeping garbage off the streets, by keeping biodegradable. 'Wet' kitchen and food wastes unmixed and separate from recyclable 'dry' wastes and other hazardous wastes, participating in primary collection of waste, using community bins for storage of waste generated in multistoried buildings, societies, commercial complexes and slums. If the reasons for doing so are extended public participation is bound to improve.

A series of measures can be taken to bring about a change in public behaviour through public awareness programmes, which could be as under.

Promote "Reduce, Reuse and Re-cycle R-R-R" of Waste

Reduce

Everyone is concerned with the growing problems of waste disposal in urban areas with the scare availability of land for processing and disposal of waste and environmental remediation measures becoming ever more expensive. It is therefore necessary to not only think about effective ways and means to process and dispose of the waste that we generate each day, it is also essential to seriously consider how to avoid or reduce the generation of waste in the first place and to consider ways to reuse and recycle the waste, so that the least quantity of waste needs to be processed and disposed of.

While the quantity of food waste generated per capita has remained almost static, the quantity of packaging waste material and non-biodegradable waste is going up alarmingly every year. This increases the burden on local bodies to deal with the problem of non-biodegradable and non-recyclable components of waste handing up at processing and disposal sites.

The following measures are therefore proposed to be taken to reduce, reuse and recycling of waste by all concerned:

(*i*) All manufactures producing a variety of domestic and non-domestic products, food as well as non-food should be persuaded to seriously endeavour to reusable packaging materials so that after the delivery of goods, the packaging materials could be collected back and use over and over again. They could also consider minimizing or avoiding use of unnecessary packaging material by innovative methods.

(*ii*) Incentives and product discount should be given to consumers for the return of packaging or bottling materials in good condition, to the waste producers or retailers to promote re-use.

(*iii*) The cost of packed articles and article without the packaging material could be kept different with a choice to the consumers to take the article without the packaging material at low cost.

Re-use

One person's waste can be useful material for other. Efforts should therefore be made to encourage collection of such re-usable material through waste collectors, waste producers, NGOs and private sector instead of allowing reusable waste to land up on the disposal site, bottles, cans, tins, drums and cartons can be reused.

Re-cycling

In the era of excessive packaging materials being used a lot of recyclable material is generated. All out efforts are necessary to retrive recyclable materials from the households, shops and establishments and fed to be the recycling industries through intermediaries such as waste purchasers, waste collectors/NGOs etc.

Promote Public Participation in SWM Systems Adopted

The first and foremost thing that the citizens need to be hold and made to understand is that no waste shall be thrown on the street, drains, water bodies, open spaces, etc. and that they should form habit of:

- Storage of segregated waste at source
- Participation in primary collection of waste
- Handling over of recyclable waste material to rag pickers/ waste collectors
- Use of community bins wherever directed/provided
- Use of litter-bins on roads and public places

Provide Information Hot-time

The key to success of any public education, awareness and motivation programme is to provide as many ways as possible for the public to interact, as promptly and conveniently as possible with policy makers, to seek clarification of doubts, share ideas or give suggestions which are constructively followed up. A telephone hot line or post box number for written communications could be one of the ways to have inputs from members of the public. The phone must be attended during working hours by police, responsive and dynamic persons who are well informed interested in the subject and available at all stated times.

Public Education

The communication material developed should be utilized in public awareness programs through variety of approaches as under:

(*i*) Group education—This may be done through:

(*a*) Group meetings in the community

(*b*) Workshops

(*c*) Exhibitions

(*d*) Lecture series

(*e*) Panel discussions etc.

(*ii*) *Mass Education* : This is very essential to cover the entire population as it is not possible to reach all the people through group education programmes.

Mass education programmes can be planned using following methods of communication.

- Use of Print Media
- Use of TV/Cable TV/Radio
- Use of cinema halls
- Street plays, puppet shows etc.
- Posters
- Pamphlets
- Use of Hoarding
- Use of Public Transport System
- Use of Primary Education Institutions/School children
- Resident associations
- NGO involvement.

NGO/Private Sector Participation

SWM services are highly labour intensive on account of increased wage structure of the Govt. and municipal employees. This service is becoming more and more expensive. Besides, the efficiency of the labour force employed in the urban local bodies is far satisfactory. High wage structure and inefficiency of the work force results into the steep rise in the cost of service and yet the people at large are not satisfied with the level of service being provided by the urban local bodies. Efforts to increase the efficiency by H.R.D and institutional strengthening will, to some extent improve the performance but they may not be enough. It is therefore, necessary that the local bodies seriously consider NGO/Private sector participation in SWM.

Private sector participation or public private participation may be considered by U.L.Bs. keeping in mind the provision of the contract labour (Regulation and Abolition) Act 1970 of the Government of India which does not permit contracting out the services already being provided by the U.L.Bs. Therefore, while considering any measure of privati/ation it is necessary to keep in mind the provisions of the above law and consider private sector participation in those areas where Municipal Corporations or municipalities are not currently providing or service. This will check growth in the establishment costs, bring in economy in expenditure and introduce an element of healthy competition between the private sector and the public sector in SWM services. There should be a right mix of private sector and public sector participation to ensure that there is no exploitation of labour as well as of the management.

NGO/Private sector participation can, therefore, be considered in newly developed areas, under-served areas and particularly in areas where local bodies have not been providing service.

NGO/Private sector participation should be encouraged in the areas of door to door collection of domestic waste door to door. Collection of commercial waste, door to door collection of hospital waste, hotel waste, construction waste and yard waste and in the area of awareness and getting public participation. The private sector may also be encouraged to set up; operate and maintain compost plants and other treatment plants and common disposal facilities. Supplying vehicles on rent, supplying vehicles on lease, repairs and maintenance of vehicles at private garbage are also some area where the private sector can be involved.

Encouragement to NGOs and Waste Collector Co-operatives

NGOs may fully involved in creating public awareness and encouraging public participation in SWM planning and practice.

The local body may also encourage NGOs are co-operative of rag pickers to enter this field and organize rag pickers in door step collection of waste and provide them an opportunity to improve their working conditions and income. The local body can give incentives to NGOs in their effort of organizing rag pickers in primary collection of recyclable and/or organic waste, and provide financial and logistic support to the extent possible.

Incentives to the Private Sector

SWM, processing and disposal is an area where the private sector has still not shown much interest. The private sector has, therefore, to be given some incentives byway of long term contract, assured supply of garbage at the plant site lease of land at nominal rates for entering this field.

NGO as well as private sector participation may be encouraged in such a way that is does not effect the interests of the existing labour, it does not violate the provisions of the above law, does not exploit the private labour and yet reduces the burden of the ULB This will substantially help in improving the quality of service of the ULBs, effect economy in expenditure and also give scope to the private sector to enter the waste management market.

Index

D

E